FOREVER TWO WHEELS

LOUDEST
FASTEST

<1%>ER

CUSTOM
MOTORCYCLES

HIGH
SPEED
THRILLS

· AND ·

LOUDEST

FASTEST

QUICK & DIRTY

MC 1%ER LOW
BROW

Outlaw

GREATEST ONE-PERCENTER

Myths, Mysteries & Rumors REVEALED

BILL HAYES

Quarto is the authority on a wide range of topics.

Quarto educates, entertains and enriches the lives of our readers—enthusiasts and lovers of hands-on living.

www.quartoknows.com

First published in 2016 by Motorbooks, an imprint of Quarto Publishing Group USA Inc., 400 First Avenue North, Suite 400, Minneapolis, MN 55401 USA.
Telephone: (612) 344-8100 Fax: (612) 344-8692

quartoknows.com
Visit our blogs at quartoknows.com

Motorbooks titles are also available at discounts in bulk quantity for industrial or sales-promotional use. For details contact the Special Sales Manager at Quarto Publishing Group USA Inc., 400 First Avenue North, Suite 400, Minneapolis, MN 55401 USA.

10 9 8 7 6 5 4 3 2 1

ISBN: 978-0-7603-4977-9

Acquiring Editor: **Darwin Holmstrom**
Project Manager: **Madeleine Vasaly**
Art Director: **Cindy Samargia Laun**
Cover Design: **Kent Jensen**
Book Design and Layout: **John Sticha**

On the front cover: **Photo by Michael Lichter**

Printed in China

TABLE OF CONTENTS

INTRODUCTION

The ratings for the series finale of *Sons of Anarchy* were bigger than an Arlen Ness fender and wider in scope than Rosie O's rear end on a '60s p-pad. The "live-plus-3" ratings (a tracking of viewers within the first three days of an original airing) racked up a total of 9.26 million insiders, outsiders, vicarious thrill-seekers, vexed-up voyeurs, bitter cops, blood-hungry hardcores, and wish-I-could-be-like-Jax wannabees jumping on for the show's last ride.

And long before the cataclysmic curtain-closing of *SOA*, an average of 7.54 million viewers were steering their remotes into each and every episode.

For good or ill, the show definitely had an impact.

But since the 1930s and '40s, the actual lifestyle that gave birth to TV's *Sons* has spawned so much more than just fertile mulch for the media. It's a secretive subculture with a spell of worldwide seduction. The few who can commit to it discover a fiery path toward a pure power and freedom that eludes virtually everyone else.

That commitment, however, is anything but easy. It's tough, macho, dangerous, mysterious, and heavily loaded with anti-hero hedonism; it's the perfect cryptic combination to hook imaginations. The life that the boys of SAMCRO speed-slammed into their weekly timeslot—and that of their counterparts in the real world—is a trip so many dream of taking.

Especially now.

The biker/one-percenter/outlaw way of life is unlike any other in modern civilized society—mainly because it's *not* modern and it's *not* civilized. It prefers fast freedom on an open road over Facebook; an attitude of FTW over a bending acceptance of every rule and law designed to keep us safe from ourselves. And by the very nature of that inherently dangerous definition, it bleeds with myths, mysteries, rumors, and lurid lore.

That's just how it works.

No rebel or revolutionary ever comes out unscathed—nor are they easily understood.

This book explores the shadows and strangeness of the innermost circles of the biker lifestyle: the clout of the clubs, the culture's wild history, intriguing international "incidents," law and disorder behind badges, mysteries within the machine, and the power-charged cult of personality that has risen (and fallen) within the outlaw world's righteous ranks.

This exploration digs deep into some of the legendary, well-worn topics—such as the 1947 Hollister "riots," the 1964 war between California's attorney general and anyone on a bike, and the bizarre and bloody relationship between Charles Manson and the Straight Satans MC.

It also turns the high beam toward new and never-ending mysteries: the continued club chaos in Australia, the feds' still-vicious vendetta to seize club patches, three-piece-patch cop clubs, the *SOA* cast on their own bikes, and many more myths and rumors "trending" today.

Both looks are needed to effectively gaze into the guts of this lifestyle. But an exhumation of the past may be the *most* important for a couple of reasons. First, legends and the questions that linger around them always lead to even more questions, which intensifies the curiosity, demanding even deeper probes. Second, this loud-piped underground universe is always in motion. It's a crazed, speeding carousel that has a core of tireless riders ringed by a wide perimeter of newbies who jump on (and sometimes off) as the circle speeds by.

This is very apparent in the first mystery that this book blasts into. Putt number one heads into the history of Nevada's Laughlin River Run, a decades-old event that has quite the past—a past that, yes, includes the 2002 shootings. That incident generated long-rolling ripples—tsunamis, really—that inundated so much of the culture with destruction and debris. Yet a recent poll of attendees at the latest incarnation of the event showed that many were clueless as to what had even happened there in '02.

That may be startling and unsettling to those who do remember—but it does prove that the lifestyle continues to receive infusions of new blood. A decaying attrition has never been a danger in this lifestyle of hyper-attraction and attention. And that's all good—just as long, of course, as the new blood is willing to accept regular transfusions from the old: transfusions of history, experience, advice, and the wisdom of age.

The myths, mysteries, and rumors that haunt this book will grip both camps. The revisited history will re-enlighten the old and educate the new; the latter-day lunacy will cruise comfortably with both.

Jax and Clay and the rest of the boys from Charming may have lit up television screens for seven seasons of made-up mayhem, but fact is always far freakier than fiction. For generation after generation, *real* one-percenters, outlaws, pioneers, outcasts, and some very legitimate loose cannons have led an existence that flattens fiction like roadkill. Their sometimes-hot, sometimes-cold blood courses with an ever-irregular pulse, and the societal puzzles they have assembled—and torn apart—were never meant to fit neatly together.

This book pours out the pieces of those puzzles and scatters them along a path that is fascinating to follow but possessed of twists, turns, and the occasional *very* dead end. Yet it's the prime passageway to a revelation of just what's under the leather, beneath the tires, on the streets, in the cells, stitched across the back, tattooed on the flesh, driving the psyche, and elevating the emotions of the cast of a cultural reality that will hopefully never experience *its* series finale.

PART 1

The Clubs

CHAPTER 1:

THE LOST LORE OF THE LAUGHLIN RIVER RUN

FROM BUTTERFLIES TO BLOOD

INTERROGATING THE SUBJECT

Will the mysteries of the 2002 Laughlin River Run Riot ever
be resolved? And does anyone remember or care, or has Laughlin's
legacy faded to pale like a worn-out pair of Levi's?

The strict "no colors" policy that has been in effect since the 2002
River Run Riot when a battle…left three dead and 13 critically injured
really has worked for the past decade. In fact, most of the vendors
and attendees that we polled didn't even know about the riot.

—motorcyclepowersportsnews.com, June 2014

The different layers in the biker world often ooze and shift like the tiers of a cheap off-the-shelf wedding cake. Distance and separation can easily cause cracks and fissures between the hardcore foundation and the ever-slipping fluff around the edges.

The Laughlin River Run is the perfect example of this dysfunctional dichotomy. It's a seven-layer bonanza when it comes to myths, mysteries, and rumors that swirl in a social batter of clubs, cops, corporate power, wrinkled road dogs, rookie riders, and violence.

Established in 1983, the run is an annual springtime soiree along the Nevada-California leg of the Colorado River. Latter-day "vendors and attendees" may not "know about the riot"—or anything else concerning Laughlin's long, strange history—but the mess that spilled out of the event's twentieth anniversary in April 2002 remains hot and steamy. The violence of that weekend and its complex aftermath continues to affect everyone who rides and rolls into major public party-downs—whether they're aware of it or not.

CRUISIN' WITH CRICKETS AND BUTTERFLIES

The Laughlin River Run began simply enough. It was the easy times of the early '80s, and San Bernardino, California, Harley-Davidson dealer Dale Marschke put together a ride to the still-fairly-small Nevada gambling outpost of Laughlin. A little over four hundred riders showed up. In the years following—like so many other parts of the biker lifestyle—it began to grow. And grow.

So did the town.

About ninety miles south of Las Vegas, Laughlin was becoming more and more popular as a low-budget-friendly, poor man's Sin City. Marschke's modest bike blast was soon one of the largest runs on the West Coast. And, dammit, it was fun. Even though the cross-the-desert ride from any nearby Nevada, California, or Arizona urban area was often an ordeal—hotter-than-hell, windy, dusty, long lines at the few and remote fuel stops—you knew you'd eventually come to a weekend finish line of comfortably cheap food and drinks, music, bikes, babes, and an old school swingin' time. For clubs and independents alike, it was all good.

The gaudy and pretty-in-pink Flamingo Hotel was always a club-friendly favorite. It was also the best venue for classic rock concerts at its riverside amphitheater. Blues bands played in big tents outside the casinos during the day for the price of a drink. Bad bikes paraded and roared with burnouts along Casino Drive. Chicks flashed, and cops were pretty laid back.

God threw down a heavy hand now and then, though. The desert that surrounds Laughlin may not be in quite the same sand league as Egypt, but the "plagues" that swooped in were at times near-biblical. Like the Year of the Crickets, when you heard horrible crunching beneath your feet with every step you took. Then the Butterfly Judgment was cast upon the land, as the yellow-gutted critters committed mass suicide by the zillions, fluttering head-on into the path of speeding bikes. Everyone pulling into town looked as though they had been squirted with fast-food mustard packets.

But, dammit, it was fun . . .

So was the proximity to old Route 66. You could roll into a time warp. Motor back to a simpler time. Hang onto at least a little bit of American heartland history.

Laughlin had it all—for a while.

FIRST BLOOD

The initial sign from the authorities that these bikers were having *too* much fun came swiftly, in the form of yet another plague—this one was set into motion by the hands of man. After years of freewheeling around the Laughlin/Bullhead City area, riders were now greeted by an intense, motorcycle-focused sobriety checkpoint as they passed in and out of the legendary town of Oatman, Arizona.

Oatman is thirty-five miles from Laughlin, along remnants of "Main Street USA," Route 66. A jaunt out there provides a good look into the back story of that curious corner of Arizona, when locals shared beer with street-staggering burros and the Oatman Hotel was the hot honeymoon spot for Clark Gable and Carole Lombard. The old inn still houses a museum's worth of memorabilia and—according to many—some highly active ghosts.

But that storied chunk of Route 66 was the *only* paved road to and from Oatman: the ideal box canyon for an authoritarian ambush. The fun-in-the-sun ride to have a brew or two amid cool 1900s Americana ambience and friendly spooks suddenly produced a potential for legal disaster.

Laughlin's fun quotient was going down—fast. Police presence all throughout the area increased. The de facto bike parade that turned Casino Drive into a nonstop showcase for chrome and craziness was no longer being "tolerated." Neither was any degree of decency-destroying nudity.

With the evils of beer consumption, bike-cruising, and boob-flashing quashed under the legal thumb, big business added a few restrictions of its own. In a move similar to ticket brokers buying up every seat for a concert, a corporate beast swallowed up all the hotel rooms in town. Rooms were now tied to packages that required multi-night stays, and the fees were fat. But hey, at least you got a free bandana.

The mystery of how a once old school, from-humble-beginnings bike run morphed into a law-loaded money-monster remains a sad head-shaker—at least, of course, for those who remember.

But the Laughlin River Run—and its many compliant, still-loyal attendees—hadn't seen anything yet.

"BAM, BAM, BAM!"

April 2002.

Happy twentieth anniversary!

In spite of its irritating and ever-increasing ills, Laughlin's big bike ball continued to survive and thrive. The crowd mix remained intact; clubs and colors were still prevalent and permitted. But the attitudes and quantities of cops made it apparent that the overall welcome warmth for the MCs was beginning to chill.

And that may have been an omen.

A little after 2:00 a.m. on Saturday, April 27, everything boiled over. The Laughlin River Run exploded into ninety seconds of blood, blades, bludgeons, and bullets.

And while the first news reports were fairly objective, the whos, whats, whens, wheres, whys, and hows would soon be replaced with those myths, mysteries, and rumors that have never been completely solved:

> Rival motorcycle gangs armed with guns and knives clashed on a crowded casino floor early Saturday, leaving three dead and at least 12 wounded as terrified gamblers ducked for cover.
>
> The shooting, the worst ever inside a Nevada casino, occurred during a weekend gathering of motorcycle groups....
>
> Denise Massey, 48, was gambling with her fiancé on the first floor of Harrah's when she noticed 20 to 30 bikers suddenly converge.
>
> "Next thing you know you just hear 'Bam, bam, bam,'" she said. "All of a sudden they're running and just shooting at each other....
>
> Sixty to 70 people, armed with guns and knives, were involved in the violence inside the entrance to Harrah's casino, authorities said.
>
> All three of the dead were bikers, police said....
>
> —Angie Wagner, Associated Press, Sunday, April 28, 2002

Harrah's was quickly locked down by the local law, Las Vegas Metro. If you were inside, you weren't getting out; if you were outside, you weren't getting back in. Period. Not until at least *some* of this had begun to be sorted out.

The cops began their process. Initial reports claimed that at least two hundred people would be "interviewed" as to what they had seen. That would take some time.

Guests inside were ordered to stay in their rooms; food would be sent up to some of the tenants-in-limbo. Husbands, wives, and friends could be seen waving and shrugging from their hotel room windows to loved ones down on the street.

Fox News reported that those inside the casino were finally allowed to leave six hours later, at around 8:00 a.m., walking around covered-up bodies in the process. CNN said that it took until 5:00 p.m. before "the hotel towers, three restaurants, and one of the casinos had reopened."

When those barriers came down, the normal, relaxing rides home became desperate escapes from a cage.

> Thousands of bikers rumbled out of town Sunday as investigators sorted out the details of a casino brawl between rival motorcycle gangs that left three people dead.
>
> Dozens of extra police patrolled the streets to guard against possible gang retaliation at one of the nation's largest motorcycle festivals.
>
> "It's just a mass exodus," said Sgt. Chuck Jones of the Las Vegas police department...If you go on the highway right now, it's just motorcycle after motorcycle as far as you can see."
>
> —Associated Press, Monday, April 29, 2002

A BEWILDERING BODY IN BFE

One of the first tangled riddles in all this—other than how everything went south in the first place—came just about an hour after the initial shootings. A body and the bike of another shooting victim—a member of one of the rivaling clubs—was found in a ravine alongside I-40 near the town of Ludlow, one-hundred-plus-miles from Laughlin. Through an apparent bit of contortion, he had been blown off his bike by being shot multiple times in the back at point-blank range. His driver's license had reportedly been set on the seat of his wrecked Harley as if to send some kind of message—but what? And to whom?

The killer—or killers—has never been found.

As late as 2011, the San Bernardino County Sheriff-Coroner's Department was still circulating cold-case notices, the murder seemingly frozen in the time-trap that is the Laughlin shootings. After so many years, the questions keep festering: like, why was that club member riding alone at that hour of the morning in an area well-known for its desolateness? And the timeline has him leaving the Laughlin area well before the 2:00 a.m. killings, so where is *that* connection? But then again, news like a casino shooting travels fast—maybe even faster than a Harley on a straight BFE road in the middle of the night.

However, some have speculated that the Ludlow death wasn't related to the riot at all; that it may have been a macabre coincidence. Other theories were explored *in depth*.

In the summer of 2003, federal wiretaps led to indictments of seventeen people in San Diego, including some who were allegedly conspiring to kill another biker who had supposedly bragged about his role in the Ludlow shooting.

At this point, it appears that the only person who knows for sure who the murderer was is the one who pulled the trigger. Shot in the back, the victim himself may not have seen the hit man, let alone recognized him.

And, yes, the 'Berdoo Sheriff's cold-case flyers still float around.

LEGAL LINGERINGS

Back in Laughlin after the wounded were tended to, the blood mopped up, and the hotel doors reopened, the official stats came down. Three were dead and CNN reported fifteen wounded, with five hospitalized: one in critical condition, three in serious condition, and one in fair condition, "all with gunshot or stab wounds."

Nine guns and sixty-five knives were gathered by cops in and around the casino.

A reported two hundred to five hundred people were involved in the long interview process.

Forty-plus arrests occurred as time went on.

As time went on . . .

From the instant that first shot was fired, it appeared that anyone and everyone connected in any way would be a permanent fixture in the Nevada and federal court systems.

In December 2003, another federal indictment was issued against forty-two individuals, charging them with ten counts of violence in aid of racketeering and one count of using and carrying firearms.

In April 2004, the second anniversary was "celebrated" as nine defendants were nailed in a seventy-three-count indictment with charges ranging from murder and attempted murder to battery, conspiracy, and assault for the purposes of enhancing a criminal gang.

In 2006, charges against thirty-six people were dismissed but six others were sentenced to prison after entering plea deals. And this is where the mysteries, myths, and rumors of Laughlin 2002 start to meld with the slow-motion of the judicial system.

The years were dragging on.

In 2007, six more pled guilty to various state felony charges, avoiding trial on charges including murder, attempted murder, conspiracy, battery, and assault that could have carried sentences of up to life in prison. Most were sentenced to prison terms ranging from two and a half to five years. Two others were sentenced in 2007, getting two years, mainly as a result of what was captured on the casino's surveillance tapes (that legendary black-and-white video footage that still pruriently pulsates around the Internet with more pulling-power than the Kennedy-Zapruder film.)

LOST IN STATUTORY SPACE

Back when the original indictments were handed out, one of the defendants immediately dropped out of sight, vanishing into an escape-ether that completely baffled the cops.

"Essentially, he disappeared off the face of the Earth for the last five years," Assistant US Attorney Eric Johnson was reported as saying.

Finally, for reasons that fall into the thick what-we'll-probably-never-know-about-Laughlin file, in July 2008, the vanished club member turned himself in. After he materialized, he was soon on his way to prison for thirty months. It was the final statutory door-slam, closing on the last of those to face federal charges in the 2002 Laughlin River Run "riot."

Of course, the deck was still being shuffled down at the civil end of the table. Laughlin law's slow hand was still being played.

WHAT DID THEY KNOW AND WHEN DID THEY KNOW IT?

In the world of civil suits, all had not remained, well, civil.

In November 2010, a Nevada jury found Harrah's Laughlin liable for injuries sustained by bystanders back in '02. Citizens caught in the casino crossfire claimed a variety of physical and emotional issues as a result of the hotel's negligence. A Vietnam vet said he had to dive off his gaming chair to take cover when the casino's "Incoming!" began. That allegedly caused a back injury and triggered emotional trauma as well as flashbacks to his combat days.

The real interesting jump in the case, though, was when the attorneys for the bystanders claimed that Harrah's had been given "information" and "intelligence" that the confrontation was imminent, and that Harrah's failed to act.

Harrah's disputed those assertions, of course, but the question remains: was the incident just a quick-fire, spur-of-a-hot-moment fight, or had there been a long, loud, and discordant orchestration in the works?

And by whom?

RAISING CAINE

One strange and seamy scenario comes from a very unlikely source; unlikely from the standpoint of truth because this source's entire "professional" life has been based upon deception and stone-stoic lies. Undercover infiltrator-for-hire and author Alex Caine lays out an eyebrow-raising, steep-slanted tale in his book, fittingly entitled *Befriend and Betray*. Caine, while involved in yet another of those near-daily attempted infiltrations of a motorcycle club, describes in deadly detail how a mix of DEA, ATF, and other alphabet-driven law enforcement agencies headed out into the desert south of Laughlin to stir up some shit. According to him, they orchestrated a serious pitting of one club against another under the very deep "color" of authority, wrapping themselves in club colors and ink, and engaging in overt/covert killings.

His tale laid out a lot to absorb.

But along with Caine, some of the most infamous slitherers in the undercover underground were also there in Laughlin 2002, including ATF agents John Ciccone and Jay Dobyns. Perhaps, with that crowd of excrement-slingers, the explosive dramatics of tainted tattoos and avengement-inciting ambushes weren't even necessary. Whispered rumors, lurid leaks in information, and any number of seedy seeds could have been primed and planted, taking deep root in raising the riot.

Did the cops really set all this up? Who killed the lone biker in the middle of the night out on I-40? Are all of the court battles—civil and criminal—finally over? When do you know when Alex Caine is lying? In a throwback to the Pearl Harbor advance-warning conspiracies, did Harrah's receive info they chose to ignore?

Ultimately, a statement made by Las Vegas police lieutenant Vince Cannito a day after the shootings may perfectly sum up the cryptic chronicle of Laughlin 2002: "Blow by blow, stab by stab, and shot by shot, we know exactly what happened in that casino. If there is any other event that precipitated what happened in there, we may never know."

The guy is right.

THE MYSTERY OF THE DISAPPEARING DRAMA

For a while, news and commentary about subsequent River Runs relived the shootings and mentioned what anniversary of the riot it was.

Eventually, though, the articles became more focused on attendance figures; only referring back to the "incident" as the cause of the lower post-2002 crowds. But the details of those early-morning moments in Harrah's were drying up in favor of economic explications.

The impact of what happened, however, hasn't dried up.

The heaviness of the Laughlin Riot landed on the entire biker culture like the dead weight of a dropped corpse. Immediately, many long-running annual gatherings, such as the Exceptional Children's Foundation charity event in Ventura, were canceled. "No

Colors Allowed" signs went up quickly, from Laughlin proper to the infinite edges of a universal perimeter, like Smokey Bear fire-warning posters anywhere and everywhere there are trees.

Restrictions on what vendors could sell at events were tightened up to exclude the evil promotion of motorcycle clubs. The old-school aura of a genuine biker weekend was sent to the principal's office for an attitude adjustment, and those in charge were more than giddy to hand out swats and punishment.

And it has apparently worked.

"I started covering Laughlin in 2009," says veteran *Thunder Press* magazine writer and bureau chief P. J. Hyland. "I noticed a significant diminution in police presence and a mellowing attitude two years ago. The storm trooper tactics employed by law enforcement after the shoot-out at Harrah's in 2002 have all but vanished."

Apparently, we now have bluebirds, rainbows, and a gentler, kinder River Run.

And that's fine—sort of. No one really wants to dodge bullets while they're drinking a free Jack-and-Coke, deciding if they should hit that sixteen or not. But the idea that the latest new-wave layer of motorcycle enthusiasts in Laughlin "didn't even know" about the jagged history of 2002 and the spiraling years that preceded it is somewhat disturbing; and a mystery in itself. Especially when it comes down to what used to be the meatiness of this lifestyle—the tough but tasty gristle that it was founded upon.

Homogenized and pasteurized milk from the most contented Guernsey may be healthier than hell for you, but any way you look at it it's still only milk. Savoring a real bite of life involves grinding that animal up. Few bikers ever need milk with a good old-fashioned hot and juicy hamburger.

REACTION AND RESPONSE

The mysteries of the Laughlin shootings have been gnawed to the bone by the clubs, by the media, by law enforcement, by infiltrators, and by witnesses; it seems unlikely at this point that any more fresh meat will be bared. Although the decades-old Laughlin River Run was once a monster in terms of attendance, its rich and strange past—a past that has had a lasting impact on all of biker culture—is definitely fading. Perhaps that's because Laughlin isn't as well-known as Sturgis, Daytona, Laconia, or even Hollister; or maybe it's just because newer riders are far more comfortable living in a purring moment than trying to understand a growling past.

It's hard to believe that the long, strange history of Nevada's Laughlin River Run—including the high-impact 2002 event—is unknown to many newbies.
Bill Hayes

CHAPTER 2:

1% DOESN'T MEAN 100% WHITE
MANY COLORS WEAR MC COLORS

INTERROGATING THE SUBJECT
Tell us the truth: Aren't all outlaw MCs "whites only"?

> I don't give a damn about your color or nationality. What concerns me
> is that when it comes time to stand up I want to know what the guy on
> the left and right of me are going to do...you say you're my brother, now
> let's go to bat here...let's put our backs together and let's do this.
>
> —"Tramp," Wheels of Soul MC

Political correctness permeates the twenty-first century. The Confederate flag has been shredded; the Washington Redskins' name has been gang-tackled; and we're all encouraged to choose the gender in which we are most comfortable, not necessarily the one that most corresponds to our plumbing. Unquestioned acceptance of de-offensification in all situations at all times appears to be the modern definition of civilized enlightenment in a refined society.

Yeah, okay, but not in the biker world.

Wide open doors of blind acceptance and compliant refinement are the evil-most enemies of any rebel lifestyle. The more mainstream society neutralizes itself, the more rebellion digs in. Not everyone believes in ignoring reality, and not everyone believes that the complete taming of society is a good thing.

But rebellion and rules-rejection in one-percenter society cover a wide spectrum. Clear-cut, day-to-day crusades, such as helmet law battles and the love of loud pipes are on one end; while the fiery, complex, and always-volatile subject of race relations is way down at the other.

Censoring the name of a football team, waving a rainbow flag, or apologizing again for the Civil War doesn't cut any hard ice when MCs face off and *discuss* things.

RIDING DOWN A VERY DIVIDED HIGHWAY

The post–World War II years produced an era of heavy de facto segregation along America's West Coast, where this lifestyle really got booming. Biker birds-of-a-feather flocked in tight tribal formation in the 1940s, and the airspace above and around the first motorcycle clubs was more than predominately white. That's just the way it was.

By the 1950s, however, the Harley horizon expanded—geographically and culturally.

> The Star Riders had been around as a riding club for a long time. They
> had chapters in Los Angeles and Oakland and were made up mostly
> of older black guys, plus a few women riders. As a carry-over from
> their military days, the Star Riders' members wore spiffy matching
> uniforms.... [The Berkeley Tigers] pre-dated the Star Riders and was

originally a drill team. They wore colors on their backs and slick green and yellow sweaters with their names embroidered on the front.... One of the earliest black clubs in northern California was the Bay View Rockets, which started up in 1951. There were also the Buffalo Riders, the Space Riders, the Jolly Riders, the Peacemakers, and the Safari Riders.... There were also the Roadrunners out of Richmond.... Then, of course, there were the Rattlers in San Francisco.

—Tobie Gene Levingston,
Soul on Bikes: The East Bay Dragons MC and the Black Biker Set

White clubs, black clubs.
"Separate but equal."
That's just the way it was...
Along with Northern California's East Bay Dragons MC and Rattlers MC, the era witnessed the founding of other black clubs, such as the Chosen Few and the Defiant Ones in Los Angeles.

The path of de facto segregation was swerving into a long and even more decidedly divided highway in the late '50s/early '60s. Myths, mysteries, and rumors claimed that some clubs had instituted hard rules to keep their membership all-white. Some writers—of the undercover-infiltrator breed and others—have published what they claim to be "all-white" clauses in certain clubs' bylaws.

Ultimately, of course, the truth behind those legends was, is, and should remain as the internal business of the respective clubs. What became more and more *external*, however, were the outward and public signs of the overall whiteness of the MC world. Swastika and SS patches as well as Third Reich battle flags were the most obvious and in-your-face. Over time, many club veterans and old-timers have commented that the patches and flags were often displayed more for shock value than as political statements. But either way, they were successful. That kind of "shock" was hard for citizens to ignore as the racial divide got wider and wider. A crossroads was close ahead.

Coming up against an all-white wall—whether de facto or formalized—led to the founding of a number of minority-based MCs throughout the 1960s. The latter part of the decade, the hard-beating heart of the Vietnam War years, saw the Wheels of Soul MC fire up in Philadelphia, proclaiming itself to be the only racially mixed one-percent outlaw club in America.

Wheels of Soul would blaze some seriously new trails as they hit that bumpy fork in the American biker's social road.

TRAVELIN' THROUGH TIME WITH TRAMP

"What we did was not only incredible; it was a real no-no at the time. This wasn't supposed to happen!"

The experiences and words of "Tramp," a brother in the Wheels of Soul MC since 1968, are not limited to just the history of his club; they expose just how searing that fiery complexity of racial tension in the one-percenter world really is.

"Like many of the members, I am a Vietnam vet. In tune with the overall history of this lifestyle, I missed the camaraderie of the military. In the war and in Wheels of Soul, we learned to respect and love those who genuinely had our backs during the worst of times—regardless of race.

"Back in that era, most MCs *were* white—*all* white. Especially the outlaws; the ones who wear the diamond 1% patch.

"The Wheels not only broke the barrier of having black members in an outlaw club, but we were *integrated*—black *and* white! We got attacked by a lot of the white-dominant outlaw clubs. We had to continually fight to survive and to keep that diamond patch...."

WHEN WE DO GOOD, NO ONE REMEMBERS...

Times have changed—somewhat.

White clubs, black clubs.

And now, larger integrated clubs.

That's just the way it is...

But when it comes to black members' acceptance into established major MCs, the de facto past and ad hoc rules have remained the status quo.

And those established majors still get the focus.

"Even into the 2000s," Tramp says, "we are still being hurt by that assumption that all outlaw clubs are all-white. With decades of riding and history fueling our club, the media still ignores us. Nobody wants to present the positive story of a predominately black club flying a diamond and all that we've experienced and had to go through. Just last weekend, we held a big event for autistic kids and not one representative of the media showed up.

"Of course, the newspapers are always there if something goes wrong and they can trash us in their headlines. 'When we do good, no one remembers...when we do bad, no one forgets' has unfortunately become a very true motto."

What's also very true is that, even though it's not close to being as high-profile, the history of black and integrated one-percent and other outlaw clubs essentially parallels that of the whites—the eras, the motivations, the needs, the organizational structure, the power, the fun.

And the brotherhood.

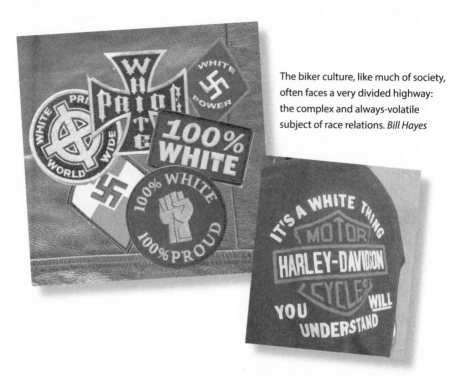

The biker culture, like much of society, often faces a very divided highway: the complex and always-volatile subject of race relations. *Bill Hayes*

Outcast MC, Ching-a-Ling MC, Buffalo Soldiers, Sin City Deciples [*sic*], Hell's Lovers, East Bay Dragons, Rattlers, Chosen Few, Defiant Ones, Wheels of Soul, and others—it's a long and growing list that proves many colors wear club colors.

But Tramp is right about the media having its eyes tightly closed to that reality; eyes that are anything but colorblind.

Published in 2007, the not-so-subtly titled *Biker Gangs and Organized Crime* got pretty emphatic as *it* leaned into the curves at those racial crossroads:

> With few exceptions, blacks are excluded from membership or riding with one-percent biker clubs. However, there are at least five black or interracial one-percent biker clubs...
>
> A possible explanation for the exclusion of blacks is that one-percent bikers are white supremacists and or racists.

But with a harsh, to-the-point "possible explanation" and a math-challenged, understated number of alternative clubs, that book took the quick-and-easy way out. In the interest of truth, the interrogation of the myths, mysteries, and rumors of club "whiteness" is just not that simple, not when you consider history and the growth of integrated clubs.

And not when you consider that blacks aren't exactly "excluded" from something that they are now a big part of.

TRUTH AND CONSEQUENCES

In 2002, filmmaker Randall Wilson produced his *Wheels of Soul* and *Glory Road* documentaries, bucking the mega mainstream media and giving rare voice to black bikers. The films have been acclaimed and they've been effective, but the big boys still have the firepower.

"Hollywood has made all of us look bad down through the years," laments Tramp.

> Look at that supposed "reality" series that was out a few years back. That caused nothing but problems for that alleged "club" and others. It showed what a lack of knowing and respecting protocol in the motorcycle club world can lead to. You don't just decide that one day you're going to put on a diamond and an MC—there are consequences to that.
>
> There are consequences to everything, really, and maybe a consequence of time and evolution is that maybe—finally—I think it's dawning on the white clubs that, "Oh hell, we're missing a lot of righteous guys out there that are black and Hispanic," and those clubs are slowly but surely beginning to take them on board—something that should have happened years ago.
>
> We may be different colors, but what makes us the elite of the elite in the biker world is that one-percent diamond patch. Now whether you like it or you don't like it, that makes us brothers. Period. That diamond patch that we all fight over and die for makes us very unique, but that also makes us brothers.
>
> But some still can't get it through their thick skulls! I say it like it is: the brotherhood aspect of this lifestyle should trump everything else!

REACTION AND RESPONSE

No. Despite patches on cuts that say things like, "100% White, 100% Proud" and "White Pride, World Wide," the one-percenter world is not an exclusively Caucasian domain. Black and integrated MCs are big and powerful, and so are the words of a veteran biker—regardless of his color—about the universal concept of brotherhood.

CHAPTER 3:

WOMEN IN THE WILD

MAMAS, SHEEP, OL' LADIES, AND LIES

INTERROGATING THE SUBJECT

So many myths, mysteries, and rumors circulate about chicks in this culture. Do ladies really love outlaws, or are they property, with some mangy wool pulled over their eyes? Or can they also be an independent but integral part of all this?

> There are few definitive statements that can be made
> about women who associate with Outlaw Motorcycle Gangs—
> women's reality in the outlaw biker subculture is yet to be fully understood.
>
> —Karen Katz,
> *Devilz Dollz: The Secret World of Women in the Outlaw Biker Subculture*

The key word in the above statement is "reality." When it comes to the ever-titillating subject of wild women, those in media readily bend and bob. They quickly shift their position from objective reporting to that of gonzo gynecologists trying to turn females and their 'cycle-society sexuality inside-out. The results usually bleed badly into botched operations that leave sensationalistic scars.

And their procedures regularly use the expired anesthesia of out-of-date data, or even worse, the slow sedative of a very tired sticker-slogan.

CHOKING ON A CLICHÉ

Early on, someone somewhere grabbed onto an easy and comfortable breakdown of "women in the outlaw biker subculture."

Something fun.

Something lilting, lyrical, and quick that apparently conveyed all there was to say about female attraction to the lifestyle.

"Ladies Love Outlaws!"

Okay, there's a valid point in that. But in embracing the bad-boy swagger of Waylon Jennings's 1972 country music classic, writers and others have spent years making the song into a sacrament. Over and over and over, they've lassoed the lyrics to elevate a romantic and hyper-poetic point. But what eased off the tongue so smoothly at first has become a highly contagious cliché that can cause choking and gagging.

Sure, Waylon was a musical outlaw giant and this cut is immortal—but damn, "Ladies Love Outlaws" became journalistically overplayed as much as oldies radio stations grind "My Girl," "My Guy," and "Do Wah Diddy Diddy" into the ground.

As poignant as Waylon's wailing and songwriter Lee Clanton's words may ultimately be, real reactions and responses condemning or clarifying women's attraction to the biker culture are not found dancing lightly around in the verses and choruses of any song.

Real reactions and responses require a serum cocktail of history, cops, over-thinking media, chicks from the day, chicks from now, and some insider MC interaction shot into a distended vein of truth.

"YOU MAY FEEL A LITTLE DISCOMFORT..."

Like it or not—and totally true or not—the first few "definitive statements" about babes-and-bikers were some of the many myths, mysteries, and rumors that author-agitator Hunter S. Thompson first fed and fueled back in 1966. Writing about "outlaw motorcycle gangs," Thompson's pioneering pen gave the world a glossary of bawdy brands and terms that included "old ladies," "mamas," "strange chicks," "pulling a train," and "turned out." Post-Thompson investigative types—media and law enforcement alike—armed with scholarly specula and well-formatted forceps, added slippery expressions like "sheep," "sweetbutts," "'property of...' patches," and lots more to the lurid list.

Their probing induced some pretty gross gushing, and the sticky mess was never-ending.

A police manual from the 1960s gave us this puddle of high-security intel:

> The females are not necessarily [club] members but at times, are close companions. There are those that are called "Mamas" that are the property of the club as a whole and will entertain any member at any time. These "Mamas" are also used to carry narcotics and run errands for members, and have been known to participate in all types of crime, including armed robbery.

The manual also had a glossary that replayed the "Mama" march and remained on a familiar track with her one-by-one-fun of "Pulling a Train."

In the early to mid-1970s other law enforcement training treatises continually reprised the same ol' greatest hits.

TRIANGULATING GENDER ROLES, SCHOLARS, AND SWEETBUTTS!

Fast-forward to the 2000s, and we find latter-day scholars and law enforcement perennially stuck in the past. You can almost hear everyone singing "Let's Do the Time Warp Again."

Thumbing through a few more pages of 2007's near-transcendental *Biker Gangs and Organized Crime*, we find a highly-detailed discussion of "Females in the Biker Subculture." The author was comfortable citing a study from 1980 (when Jimmy Carter was president and people were buying Captain and Tennille LPs) that said "the status of women in the biker subculture was not much different from their status in the lower-class culture from which they came. They had low self-concepts compatible with their status as bikers' old ladies. Even though one-percenters did not hide their contempt for females, there was an adequate supply of women, who were primarily looking for excitement. The females were often as tough and hard-bitten as the bikers...."

Lower-class, low self-concepts, contempt, hard-bitten...an apparent tone was being set.

Then the book jumped all the way to a study from later in the '80s (when Reagan had the reins and David Lee Roth had hair). It was a "study of gender roles and the norms governing them in one-percent biker clubs [that] is among the first of its kind in scholarly literature. Using a triangulation methodology—informal interviews with law enforcers, current and former bikers, and current and former female consorts; review of journalistic and scholarly articles; and participant reflection—[the study conductor] identified three distinct status roles for females in the biker subculture: mamas, sweetbutts, and old ladies."

Gender roles?
Triangulation methods?
Sweetbutts?
WTF?!

THROW MAMA FROM THAT DAMN TRAIN ALREADY!

Meanwhile, a 2008 educational exposé about OMGs (Outlaw Motorcycle Gangs) was produced by the sheriff's department of one of America's largest cities. It featured, of course, a section on women's involvement with the clubs. The stench of oft-recycled revelations was getting even more stale:

MEMBERSHIP REQUIREMENTS—FEMALES

- [The women] are often called "Mamas" or "Sheep" and are considered property of the club to be shared by all. An exception to the property classification is made for wife's [*sic*] and girlfriends (Old Ladies) of individual members.
- Many clubs will allow the females to wear a club patch with the words "Property of" underneath it.
- Many work as prostitutes or in strip bars and hustle drugs for the gang.
- They will hold weapons and drugs for the gang on bike runs.

Staccato police jargon and scholar-speak may sound like the jumbled disclaimer at the end of a radio commercial, but evidently just-the-facts-ma'am and "triangulating" sweetbutt scuttlebutt has helped some people to sort out just where they think women fit into the biker wild.

Some people.

The truth about women's connection to biker culture is ultimately found in the hearts, minds, souls, words, and high-energy estrogen of the gals who have lived the life. *Archives of Bill Hayes*

A DIFFERENT BREED OF WOMEN

Right around the same time that *Biker Gangs and Organized Crime* was coordinating its "study conductors" and the big-city sheriff's office was working its workbook, pioneering filmmaker Randall Wilson was meeting the subject at street-level. He was at it again, doing what he does best: taking his cameras and skills behind rarely opened doors to present the positive—and truthful—side of the biker lifestyle.

No cop intel.

No scholarly speculation and abstract analyses.

Just real interaction with real bikers.

The result was his epic *Hessians MC,* a visceral view into the history and personal lives of the brothers—and their women—of the legendary motorcycle club.

The Hessians MC was founded in 1968, another of the clubs spawned in the screaming surroundings of the Vietnam War years. They have had plenty of time to experience this lifestyle from the inside out. Their documentary features a stark focus on females long associated with the club; it's pure and razor-straight in what it presents from well-wizened hearts, minds, and souls. In a running conversation that few if any in the mainstream would ever be invited to sit in on, a time-spanning cross-section of biker women along with a few of the members dissect then and now. Widows of veteran patch-holders from the '60s, a newer member and his young wife, and some seriously grizzled old-timers engage in some corroboration on the media's glossary of glorification—along with some heavy editorial expansion.

"Everybody called the biker woman a 'mama,'" explained Linda, a widow whose husband had been a club brother since the early years, "and that's really rather an insult to most of us because a 'mama' is somebody that goes around and screws everybody. The only girls that lasted in the Hessians are the ones that had the guts."

"Back then the girls danced in bars to pay for [their men's traffic] tickets," remembered another widow, Edith. "The girls were wild. Every battle that their old man fought, they fought. Usually they ended up with broken jaws, teeth knocked out, but they had a good time of it."

"Some of the women," Linda corroborated, "were just as totally terrifying and scary as guys!"

"More outrageous '60s and '70s behavior," reminisced loveably haggard Hessian, Guyron. "We've got one brother who had a little altercation with his wife and he scalped her like an Indian! [laughs] That's not funny [still chuckling] but he took her to the doctor and had her scalp sewed back on and she has a full head of hair and they're still together."

All's well that ends well, and sensitive reminiscing goes a long way toward setting a scene, but then things got serious again.

"It's the club, then your bike, then... let's see, were we third?" Linda asked herself, again going back in time, "You had to accept that sometimes the club was first... accept it and respect it."

"There's a lot of girls out there that just don't know how to take it," agreed Robin, the adult daughter of another veteran member. "They don't last very long a lot of times. They expect to be number one all the time but when they get with a club or a patch holder there's certain obligations and priorities they have that some women just can't take second to. It's definitely a breed of women that's different."

PROBLEMS AND PRESSURES WITH "PROPERTY OF..."

Then the women started to unravel some of the tangled threads in a symbol that the media and law enforcement has forever looked at as just one step above—or maybe below—a dog collar.

"We had our 'PO' patches for years," said Linda. "First I was, 'Oh, I'm nobody's property!' but I took it wrong. After a while it was good to have that on my back, be part of the club and the family and my husband's name back there and 'the Hessians.'"

But those tangles had some pretty tight knots, and the POs were eventually pulled.

"You know, I still see a lot of these clubs around with these 'Property of...' patches," longtime Hessian Keith revealed. "We used to have 'em. In fact, the very early ones had our center patch in them! But, my God, that turned into a can of worms.... I tell you what...some of these women are really, really vicious...they started having a thing of their own...."

And that just doesn't fly—then or now—in the one-percent MC world whose membership is still the hard-muscle milieu of men.

Women riders are seen more and more here in current and chic times. They even have clubs of their own. Not, however, within the recognized outlaw ranks.

But they've certainly experienced them.

TIME TEMPERS THE OCCASIONAL DOMESTIC SCALPING

Tender and touching as it was, Guyron's hair-raising story was juxtaposed against how things are now, nearly a couple decades into the twenty-first century.

"My grandma used to ask me," said Tina, young wife of Hessian Byron, "when I first started dating [Byron] if those stories were true that she read in books about the Hessians...about how they passed their women around. I told her, there are women who jump from men to men, but usually the righteous old ladies, they stick to their man and that's about it."

"Bottom line is," added Byron, sitting in a nice suburban house with his young son playing, "that it's not what the public perceives it to be.... We're no different than the Joneses next door, except...I ride a motorcycle."

But that motorcycle does provide a hefty degree of separation. Most of those next-door Jones folks usually find other ways to get their thrills. And, let's face it, those thrills probably have never included even the slightest connection—historical or otherwise—to good-time broken jaws, topless dancing for bail money, and the occasional domestic scalping (all of which, thankfully, society's sophisticated evolution has greatly tempered!).

That motorcycle is also a forever-centerpiece of attraction for special men—and women.

From the late 1960s to well into this era of the milquetoast Millennials, "women's reality in the outlaw biker subculture" may "yet to be fully understood" in the realm of academics, authorities, and probing journalists. But Hessian Byron's "bottom line" of the public's loopy perception of a way of life they have never actually lived is totally true—and timeless.

THE WICKED BITCH CONNECTION

Like the Hessians women, author Amy White has lived it—but in a much more independent way.

Amy is proud of her self-anointed title—and book—"Wicked Bitch."

No elusive reality exists in *her* world.

She is also proud that virtually her entire life has been one of deep personal connection to the biker culture and those who are truly a part of it.

> I adore men...I love their voices, from the crooning silk of David Allan Coe and Randy Travis to the rumbling timbered feeling of a man talking softly when I lay my head on his chest....I love them when they dress up in camouflaged clothes and hunting rifles....I adore the gentle ferocity of a war-torn Vietnam vet...and respect the unbreakable bond of brotherhood.
> —*Wicked Bitch*, 2009

And with self-interrogation, she establishes a passionate one-percent-and-woman connection.

> On my left shoulder, there is a small blue rose.... Above that rose is a tiny little 1%. The tiny, curly, pretty little symbol carries a lot more weight, significance, conversation and speculation than the dragon that covers a good half or more of the right side of my back.... There are women who assume that a 1% means I have murdered someone, or committed a felony to belong to a club. That is not what it signifies; it means to me that I am one of the 1% of the biker population for whom my Harley is my way of life....I have a family. They wear leather, tattoos and scraggly beards. They will take good care of me no matter what, and never once have any of them had to check to see how many bruises they left on my skin.

And it's a pretty safe bet that Amy's biker family has never referred to her as a "sheep," "mama," or, amazingly enough, even a "sweetbutt."

HOW HIGH CAN "WILD" GO?

Betsy Guisto has lived the life as well. In her 1997 PhD dissertation (as cited in our old favorite study guide of complexities and intricacies, *Biker Gangs and Organized Crime*), her words and thoughts are actually surprisingly straightforward. She exposes the possibility of a simple solution to at least a portion of the ladies-and-bikers riddle.

After spending twenty years involved with a major MC, in the end Betsy said that she was drawn to the biker universe "because I have always felt a strong attraction toward walking on the wild side, and the one-percenter lifestyle embodies the height to which wild can go."

Okay.

Easy to understand.

Betsy. Amy. Famed female photojournalists like Felicia Morgan, who is never off her bike. Authors like Lisa Petrocelli and Ann Ferrar. All-female clubs now number into the hundreds, riding out a lifestyle that "embodies the height to which wild can go."

The altitude adjustment just makes sense.

Male or female, the desire to ditch the mainstream mundane and take that "walk on the wild side" has been powering this way of life since the beginning.

And this power is a drug that never expires.

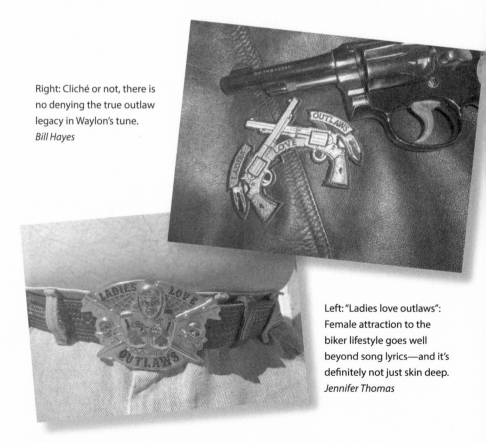

Right: Cliché or not, there is no denying the true outlaw legacy in Waylon's tune.
Bill Hayes

Left: "Ladies love outlaws": Female attraction to the biker lifestyle goes well beyond song lyrics—and it's definitely not just skin deep.
Jennifer Thomas

"WANT TO PULL A TRAIN ON A SHEEP?!"

It's a beautiful SoCal mid-summer Sunday in 2015, the day of a monster run. Riders roll from the coast to the infamous heartland of 'Berdoo, then north to the former railroad town of Mentone, fifty miles southwest of Big Bear Lake.

In 'Berdoo, they meet with several hundred members of a major MC—a club consistently designated by law enforcement as a group that "poses a serious criminal threat to those areas in which its chapters are located."

Plenty of ladies are with the pack and many more are at the final destination, a giant old-timey bar and beef joint. The women range from good-looking to drop-dead gorgeous and many wear that frequently factious fashion of "Property of..." patches.

The women in this wild bear no resemblance to those described by Hunter Thompson as "oxpeckers: small, dull-colored birds that feed on ticks that they pick from the backs of infested cattle and wild animals." There is none of the hollow-eyed sadness that supposedly permeated virtually all of the beat-down ladies of that era, suffering mightily simply because of their lust to love outlaws.

But any way you look at it, times have changed. And any pain from the past aside, the chicks at this run here and now were hot. Conversations between brothers were void of even one of those official but uncomfortable glossary tags.

"Hey, brother, want to pull a train on a sheep?! She's a real sweetbutt!" was never heard.

But what *was* seen and heard was another rich part of this way of life that cannot be defined by old drive-in movie dialogue.

Or a song.

Or replays of Thompson 1966.

Or in a "study of gender roles."

Or in a Gang Task Force textbook.

The truth about women in this lifestyle is ultimately found in the hearts, minds, souls, words, and high-energy estrogen of the girls and gals who live—and have lived—the life.

REACTION AND RESPONSE

It seems that while women who willingly roam the badlands of bikers and one-percenters have evolved since the 1960s, the official outside view of them has not. But, according to the words from many of their own sweet voices, they are no longer enslaved victims from the shadows of myths, mysteries, and rumors. Instead, they are proud of being a "different breed." And while they may "adore men," they seem to be just as adoring of taking their own personal walks on the "wild side."

CHAPTER 4:

PURPLE WINGS... REALLY?

CODES, SECRETS, AND ANTI-EVERYTHING ACRONYMS

INTERROGATING THE SUBJECT

What's with all the cloak-and-dagger stuff? Is the biker
culture neck-deep in a mysterious world of cryptic symbols, rituals, rites,
and practices? Come on, what does all that junk really mean?

Wow! Somehow you don't see many of *those* patches around.

To earn the coveted purple wings, one would certainly have to find himself in a very rare situation; a scarce scenario where everything must fall into place pretty precisely. Truly one of those right-place-at-the-right-time cases of "snatching the moment," as it were.

But damn, it would be well worth it! That few-and-far-between plum-colored patch would make for a nice addition to any biker's or one-percenter's collection of mysterious materiel; an assumed wealth of wonder that stirs up and seduces curious citizenry and law enforcement alike.

How, though, could so much covertness surround a way of life that is anything but low-profile? Since the beginning, very little has ever been toned down in the way of outlaw *expression*. Big back patches, the occasional in-public over-the-top behavior, constant media exposés, and vicious vehicles tuned for maximum sound and speed are not the stuff of a secret society.

Ultimately, the answer is found in the exclusivity of the lifestyle; anything difficult to get into opens itself up to stampedes of speculation from the outside. If one doesn't know for sure about something, one imagines. And from the lofty deck of the one-percenter's voyage through vicarious living, plenty of bait spills overboard, attracting a feeding frenzy of excited imagination.

Provocative patches with unapologetic contempt for society, graphic glimpses of shocking party-downs, hints at horrible hazing, and law enforcement's insistence that hidden weapons occupy every biker's human and mechanical orifices provide succulent bloody bits for society's sharks to nibble on. Throw in television's today-hip biker documentaries and death-dramas, a constant cult-following for old "B" 'cycle-savage movies, and books written by pissed-off ex-club members and undercover cops, and you have quite a menu.

FROM FLASH TO FUBAR

The exclusiveness in this lifestyle began, of course, with motorcycles. But graphic patches—further outward signs that bikers weren't like everyone else—quickly became part of the package. Way back in 1932, the Gypsy MC reacted to the public's perception of them as the "sour pickles of the road" by making, yes, a crazed pickle powering a bike their in-your-face back patch. The Outlaws—founded in 1935—have forever been recognized by their ominous skull center-patch. Then the big push of club-establishment in the '40s and '60s gave us more skeletons, sabers, gods, ghouls, and a palette of portraits of power.

Patches are a statement—a statement that anyone and everyone can see. A statement that the wearer *wants* anyone and everyone to see.

Independents—non-club members—have forever been "slickback" (a cut with no recognized club patch) billboards for the "flash" patches: slogan-strips that are available for anyone to buy at public events. Their acronym angst and axiom attacks include "FTW," "WTF," "BOB," "13," "RUB," and the perpetually hilarious "DILLIGAF." These, and many others, have secured a permanent place in biker glossary slang, similar to the military's FUBAR and SNAFU.

And the purpose of all these initialed-inspirations is similar, too: they're *fun*, damn it! It's a confuse-the-citizens fun that extends to—or was inspired by—club cuts. And that's where we see this fun combined with real mottoes of meaning, the identity brands, and credos people dedicate their lives to. That's where we see a confuse-the-cops style of fun.

FINE-TUNING THE DECODER RINGS

Most MC patches—the ones with words, at least—are pretty straightforward: club name, location, and the occasional mission statement. Steely sentiments like "Respect Few, Fear None" and "We Give What We Get" are just a couple that need no explanation.

But there are others.

A few phrases, acronyms, and short designations on MC cuts have set law enforcement into an anti-encryption motion that smacks of kids with cereal box decoder rings in the '60s. Authorities have dialed in that certain patches represent everything from identifying a member as someone who has killed for the club to slogans proclaiming open season on rival MCs.

Ironically, law enforcement generally applies a fairly simple definition to the very complex diamond one-percent patch. A typical official explanation reads: "The wearer considers himself to be part of the one percent of motorcyclists who are members of an outlaw motorcycle gang."

Evidently those officials need a little WD-40 on their decoder rings. No one can "consider" himself to be a member of a club; you either are or you aren't. And the original math in the legendary 1947 American Motorcycle Association (as the American Motorcyclist Association was known then) statement about "one percent of motorcyclists being the troublemakers" was directed at all early bikers in general; it was not aimed specifically at club membership numbers.

The truth is that the diamond patch may be the singular symbol *most* laced with myths, mysteries, and rumors. Its meaning—and whether it's pejorative or positive—differs greatly from club to club and often from individual to individual. Some embrace it; some don't. Plus, the "1%" diamond has become another victim of the popularization of the culture, joining other flash patches for public consumption online and at event vendor booths—right along with full sets of Sons of Anarchy colors.

Even so, a legitimate one-percent diamond on a legitimate cut always packs a lot of punch. Two-dollar swap meet patches, not so much. But hey, at least now it's easy and inexpensive for one to "consider" oneself a "Redwood Original."

FLAPPING *THOSE* WINGS AGAIN

But the patches without words are the mysteries that most pique the curiosity of the public and the police. Like field mice frantically sniffing at the small crack between a threshold and the bottom of a door, they simply have to know what's on the other side—even if they might get stepped on in the process.

At the top of the riddle list has always been those colored wings. They were another of those prurient puzzles that Hunter Thompson started to piece together in the '60s, but they have taken long flights since then.

Current cop clarifications of the raw rainbow of wings usually begin with the traditional, most infamous, most well-known, and evidently most frequently practiced:

- Red Wings means wearer had oral sex while female was menstruating.

Ho hum, been there, done that, but then it gets more and more colorful:

- Blue Wings means wearer had oral sex with a cop.
- Brown Wings means wearer had oral sex on a woman's anus.
- Green Wings means the wearer had oral sex with a woman who has a venereal disease.
- Gold Wings means wearer performed sexual relations with a woman during a gang rape involving 15 or more persons.

And yes, then there's that *special* one:

- Purple Wings means wearer had oral sex with a female corpse.

Police investigators and decoders add that all of these acts must be witnessed by other club members in order to make the wingman fully eligible for the patch. And essentially, they're right—it's a titillating twist on Reagan's "Trust, but verify!"

Authorities are quick with explanations for other cut accessories as well, with the upside-down police shield being one of the more interesting:

- Upside down Law Enforcement Badge or Patch alleges it was taken from an officer by force.

You can almost hear a very unfriendly tone of voice as you read *that* one.

THE ERROR IS IN THE INTENTION

So, once the decoding is done, then what? Once it's established that things like those wicked wings exist and that some brothers wear them, then what? Is breaking that code any more Earth-stopping than Captain Midnight's secret transmission of "Eat Your Vegetables!"?

Is there a fine line between fun and facts, or is it more of a fence with no gate to the "Zany Zone" side of the carnival? In the true crime-fighting end of things, where does the knowledge of where someone puts his tongue fit in?

Law enforcement's error may be in its intention. Sure, "Know your enemy" is a basic of warfare, but law enforcement often misses the fact that there just might be a punch line in that pursuit.

"AAMOF," at times they look just a silly as a "BGOALB."

"YKWIM?"

TAKE ME TO CHURCH

Moving on, we move into MC clubhouses, where even more myths, mysteries, and rumors ride hard into the minds and imaginations of outsiders, with no keys to those doors. Most clubhouses post a greeting like "Members and Invited Guests Only." That barrier alone gets the strong juices of wonder flowing.

But wait: millions of television viewers were invited behind the door of the SOA clubhouse, and those millions got a first-run, high-def look at a usually impenetrable inner circle. Occupied by its massive, carved boardroom-like table, SAMCRO's Charming retreat was home to scheming, savagery, and sex. Surely, the door to an inside like that, so thick with thrills, must be indicative of what's contained in all MC HQs.

Maybe.

Scheming, savagery, and sex, coupled with some steady booze-swilling, does all add up to a degree of commonality in what is found in *some* clubhouses. *A degree.* They are, after all, the refuge and workrooms for motorcycle clubs, not dorm rooms for fragile frat boys who can't hold their liquor. And clubhouses probably best even Vegas in exemplifying the old saying "What happens there, stays there."

But they are also the sanctums for "church," the generally accepted term for regularly scheduled chapter meetings. Church is a highly respectful euphemism that was popularized early on, according to the history of the Monks MC, a club established in 1963.

But is church the proper place for the ordering of dirty deeds and the hideous hazing that is alleged to befall prospects and new members?

WHILE ALL FELONS MIGHT NOT BE BIKERS...

> The prospect period is designed to make candidates show their loyalty to the club, which often includes committing crimes and participating in violent behavior. Today's outlaw biker gangs are involved in a wide range of crimes, officials say. While they've stuck with traditional moneymakers like drugs, firearms and extortion, they are starting to get involved in things like human trafficking, prostitution and even white-collar crimes like counterfeiting and money laundering. Prospects are a part of all of it—and violence is often expected by the gang.
>
> Sadly, the ultimate way for a prospect to prove his loyalty is through murder.
>
> —James King,
> "How to Join an Outlaw Biker Gang," vocativ.com, May 20, 2015

The myths, mysteries, and rumors that ricochet off of statements like these have to be examined more in terms of math than in emotion or speculation. The FBI estimates that "44,000 Americans belong to OMGs," according to its 2011 National Gang Threat Assessment; and law enforcement continually reports that "the number of OMG participants is increasing."

That would make for a lot of murders, especially considering that in 2011 and the years following, the total US homicide rate across all strata of society tallies in at somewhere around 14,000 to 16,000 per year.

Sure, being a prospect with a motorcycle club is hard work and it is definitely a period designed to demonstrate loyalty. And yes, part of that loyalty is to dispel any thoughts by members that the probate might be a law enforcement infiltrator, wired for sound and bonded to the belief of the badge rather than to the brotherhood of the MC. But clubs in the twenty-first century have technology. Extensive background checks and even Q-and-A sessions connected to a lie detector save everyone—prospect and club alike—from the unwanted police attention that unsophisticated "tests" such as random killings have a way of attracting.

But still, the 2010 sheriff's manual that introduced us to cadaver cunnilingus also stated that "Probationary members (Prospects) are ordered to use illegal narcotics and to commit felony crimes." Now, like the murder implications, this is pretty dogmatic stuff that paints with a broad bureaucratic brush, looking at an entire subculture through a variation on a profiler's pre-supposed formula: *While all felons might not be bikers, all bikers are felons.*

But that particular sheriff's department has had a few felonious hiccups of its own, lately. Nearly twenty officers, including a former undersheriff (who is also the current mayor of a city in the county) and a former captain, were indicted on federal obstruction and conspiracy charges.

Back in 2010, a group of deputies were exposed as having their own "gang" at a local jail (complete with matching tattoos and everything!), and accused of setting up gladiator-type fights between inmates, along with other abuses. Also in 2010, the department hired almost three hundred new officers. Then it was discovered, long after they'd pinned on their badges, that a third of them had lied on their applications, fifteen had cheated on their polygraph tests, and about two hundred had already been disqualified for employment by other law enforcement agencies.

One county over, *their* sheriff was finally released from federal prison in May of 2015 after serving several years on corruption charges. He was convicted, along with his wife and his "alleged" longtime mistress. A few years before *that*, the undersheriff of that county saw his seventeen year-old son convicted in the rape of an unconscious sixteen-year-old girl.

There was no mention in the media of whether or not daddy's sheriff's department was considering giving the kid *pink* wings for that one.

MOTORING UNTIL THE MOIST VOMIT-VEST HAS DRIED

Once a prospect patches in—having completed his list of murders, felonies, or other mayhem—even more myths, mysteries, and rumors kick in.

An article written in May of 2015, right after nine bikers were killed at the now-extremely infamous "massacre" in Waco, Texas, purported to give a quick "primer" on outlaw motorcycle gangs, including initiation rituals. The piece dipped that broad brush of biker-bashing into a deep bucket yet again.

Once the prospect makes the cut, they "reportedly engage in a particularly vile initiation process," in which other group members "urinate, defecate, and vomit" on the initiate's vest. "The new member would then put the now-moist vest back on, hop on his bike, and go motoring until the vest had dried."

— Tom Jacobs, "A Quick Primer on Outlaw Biker Gangs," www.psmag.com, May 18, 2015

But above the text was a photo of a club member in a cut with the kind of impeccable cleanliness that sets red carpet fashionistas into full "gush" mode. *Awkward...*

The truth about initiations in modern times is that they—like feelings about the diamond one-percent patch—vary from club to club, as they always have. There is no denying that the 1960s and '70s produced some pretty gross and gooey patch baptisms; shoeboxed stacks of old snapshots prove that. But that was a different day. Look around—and sniff around—when you go to an event with club members present. Granted, some very well-worn cuts may be found on the old-timers, but it's obvious that the days of stand-up-by-themselves-oil-riddled-Levi's and barf-battered, excrement-encrusted cuts are long gone.

Except, of course, in the mind of law enforcement and the media.

NINJAS, KNIGHTS, AND FISHHOOKS

One of the final bundles of myths, mysteries, and rumors that seed the fertile cryptic club culture has to do with how your average brother manages to arm himself. With super-stealth that would make a ninja proud, virtually every corner and crevice of the biker's person and putt is reputedly transformed into a war machine.

Beginning up close and personal, law enforcement warns its officers to "Watch out for needles, razor blades, and fishhooks in [bikers'] clothing seams during your pat-down search."

The idea of riding comfortably, walking around, or even getting dressed at all with a wardrobe that is laced with needles, razor blades, and fishhooks is disconcerting. It's like those photos you see in tattoo shop albums of multiple-pierced labia and scrotums—it makes most people nervous and curious as to how these individuals rattle and clink through normal daily living.

Added to the sharps in the trouser-tucks we now move to full-on weaponry. Officers are further warned, "Bikers have been known to stash weapons within there [*sic*] engines, on their old ladies, inside their boots, and sewn inside hidden pockets in their vests."

Wow!

This picture of motorcycle club members now painted by authorities is abstract, to say the least, like one of those what-the-hell-is-that Picasso portraits of odd perception. Because here we have this guy who is armored like a medieval knight in barbed denim, shrouded in patches that confess murders, encrusted in vomit, menstrual gore in his beard, walking gingerly out to his big bike that—again according to law enforcement—is outfitted like the Batmobile.

After the inevitable traffic stop, if an officer survives lacerations and severed arteries during the pat-down of this beast, he must then begin a thorough inspection of the bike, which may contain any or all of the following:

- Dipstick Knives (Knives disguised as an oil dipstick—don't worry about wipin' if you have to whip it out!)

- Shotgun Mounted to Motorcycle Bars (Full shotguns mounted to the handlebars and painted to blend in with the rest of the bike.)

- Hidden Tire Gauge Gun (Yep, a good old fashioned zip gun made from a tire gauge.)

- Hidden Motorcycle Handlebar Shotgun (Handlebars modified to fire a .410 shotgun shell: "This is why you should always approach a motorcyclist on his right side. The right hand grip contains a movable throttle which is much more difficult to modify.")

- Hidden Firearm in Frame-Mounted Toolbox (Glock in the box.)

- Handlebar Knife (Bar-mounted knife that blends in with the controls.)

- Hidden Firearm in Seat (Handgun placed inside of hollowed-out seat foam and then leathered over.)

- The Cracker ("Outlaw Motorcycle Gang members are incorporating a new type of improvised weapon they call the 'cracker.' They suspend a nylon whip with metal attachment from their handlebar. These 'crackers' can be quickly accessed by the rider and swung as a weapon like a ball 'n' chain.")

- Handgun in Gloves (Derringers in riding gloves: "The gun could be fired while the rider looked like they were simply putting their gloves on or off.")

- Radio Jammer (High-tech weaponry during traffic stops preventing cops from communicating with one another: "One Adam-12, do you copy? Do you copy? 10-9!")

The ever-popular, always-hilarious, and perpetually mysterious to the mainstream "DILLIGAF"!
Jennifer Thomas

Whew! With all that going on, how does this guy ever get out of his house to ride? Getting suited up unsliced, locking and loading, preparing the old lady to be harnessed up with the back-up heat, sharpening the knives, programming in the freqs on the radio jammer, and hanging that "cracker" just right for quick access sounds like an all-day job.

But maybe, just maybe, not every veteran club member regularly goes through this kind of battle-prep routine. Maybe these examples of gizmos and deadly doo-dads represent far-most extremes rather than the norm. Maybe the darkest MC secrets swirl thinly around in the pitch-black outer edges of the biker universe while the healthy normal warmth of a friendly sun remains at the center.

A SIT-DOWN WITH SPIKE

There is no better way to expose truth than to have lived it. "Spike" has been a member of the Hessians MC for over twenty years, has held many positions, including president of the club's mother chapter, and is a tireless activist and ambassador for the entire lifestyle.

He's charted every bright star, every jagged tumbling asteroid, and every other obstacle and pathway in the MC cosmos, while maintaining an unwavering orbit around the lifestyle's steady core.

"Patches, parties, prospects, and police...hmm. Well, I've always looked at the one-percenter label, and the diamond patch, as something that was bequeathed from an outside source. Our club has been recognized, of course, by police as a one-percent organization, but we don't want to participate in that nonsense, so we came up with our own tag: '100% Hessians.' But there are people who have no idea what a real one-percenter is all about, and when they *buy* the patch and put it on, they put themselves in jeopardy from cops and other sources. But they want that bad-boy image; they remind me of a clean dog that *wants* to get fleas, thinking it will make him tougher!"

BOGUS BARCODES

Law enforcement naturally represents the Black Hole in the biker galaxy, pulling everything it can into its crush, sucking out light and life!

"I find it amusing when the authorities attempt to interpret club patches," says Spike, "especially those that have no words—colored bars and the like. It drives the police crazy. It becomes like barcodes in the supermarkets, with the cops running around as if they have those little handheld pricers, trying to get a clear reading!

"But law enforcement often gets a very *unclear* reading. I've seen our very own "HFFH" patch on an official list of 'hate symbols.' Hate symbols? It means 'Hessians Forever, Forever Hessians.' When they misinterpret a patch like that, there's no doubt they'll have a problem with some of the more esoteric patches that clubs have."

NUDITY, MUD, URINE: PART OF THE PROCESS

Sometimes there will be a total eclipse, where not even a shadow can be seen. Where myths, mysteries, and rumors come alive in the void.

"What goes on behind closed doors is as diverse as the clubs and the people themselves," Spike admits.

> They're not so much a mystery as they are simply private. I've been to clubhouses worthy of being corporate boardrooms and I've been to clubhouses where more organized piles of trash exist at a waste dump. They're places to crash for less-fortunate brothers, they're comfortable retreats, and some are used as commercial enterprises. Or they're set up in a public place, like a bar, or just under a tree in a park.
>
> And sure, behind those doors can be initiations and hazing. But that sort of thing in general—be it bike clubs or at universities or elsewhere—has changed with the times. What was once acceptable is no longer. The whole initiation process had always been to have fun but at times it could also be humiliating, and how one deals with that humiliation was a part of it—building strength and character. And it can further prove how much someone wants to be a part of that organization.

In our club in the old days, the idea of nudity and mud and urine was indeed part of the process; but frankly, now you can be locked up for decades for being that exposed in a mud puddle! Something that was looked on as fun in the old days has much more serious connotations now.

But there is a bridge between the old days and today, though unfortunately it's a shaky one.

ASKING THE RIGHT PEOPLE THE RIGHT QUESTIONS

Extinction and evolution are fluid parts of any universe, but evolution is most important when it comes to moving forward. A myopic focus on what's extinct can blind someone to what's going on around them now.

"It's quite obvious and evident that police use old film footage and information to disseminate their info on motorcycle clubs and bikers," Spike states. "I am absolutely bowled over when I'm interrogated at a stop by officers armed with their current intel. With all the money and high-tech equipment that is dedicated to these organizations, they're still relying on and believing in manuals that were put together back in the '70s and '80s. Nothing has kept up with the times. You'd think that, by now, they'd realize what a crock of shit that is!

"They use hearsay, material from people who are merely self-professed experts about bikers, and random thoughts and conjecture from officers at roadside stops. This so-called 'intel' is then passed on to fusion centers as fact, instead of the right people being asked the right questions and being validated. So much of their information is a jumble, mixing in single isolated cases with things that may have been true once. I've known a lot of bikers, but I've still yet to meet one who had a gun in his handlebars or fishhooks in his clothes. I've done a lot of fishing; the only time I've ever found tackle in my pants is after a bad mistake with a poor cast!"

LADIES LOVE OUTLAWS (REPRISE)

The role of females in motorcycle gangs changed. Although earlier biker women were simply partners in parties and hedonistic sexuality, the women in modern outlaw gangs are expected to be engaged in economic pursuits for their individual men and sometimes for the entire club. The changing role of the biker women appears to be influenced by the gangs' increased involvement in crime and other money-making activities.

—C. B. Hopper, J. Moore, "Women in Outlaw Motorcycle Gangs," *Journal of Contemporary Ethnography*, January 1990

"The idea of giving guns to the old ladies and women in the middle of a melee is ridiculous!" Spike says, laughing. "So many girls now wouldn't dare break their nails or mess up their hair as they jockey to shoot over their shoulder from the back of a bike! It's still a man's world out there in this lifestyle. So many guys these days have these glamorous young chicks. It's an equation that adds up to this: the badder an individual is perceived to be, the cuter and more delicate his lady probably is! Though, of course, there are the exceptions, like the old-school old ladies."

PROSPECTING FOR PINKS

A bit of a toxic conscriptive cloud that still occasionally drifts through the MC star cluster is the rite and practice of signing one's bike over to the club. Spike addresses *that* interrogation:

> One other mystery is whether or not some clubs make you transfer your bike over to them as part of the membership process. Yes, some clubs have done that. To them, it's part of the commitment and the unwritten contract. It's like when you get a credit card and have to pay it back with interest. You promise to join a club, devote a lot of time, and give it your all. If you don't—in some environments— well, it's going to cost you your bike.
>
> I think it's really strange when you get somebody coming around the club for a long period and the brothers take the time to work with him and then suddenly he says, "No it's not for me."
>
> "Well," say some clubs, "You broke our contract and cost us a lot of time and energy, young man, and that just cost you your motorcycle."
>
> No, it's not an easy road being a prospect—whether you lose your bike or not—but when I hear law enforcement profess that every club prospect must commit felonies or murder, I cringe.
>
> And then I think back to a situation that I will never forget.

LEARNING AND LIVING—THE LIES

It was time for one final quasar from Spike—a bright blast of truth soaring above the nadir of assumption and ignorance:

> I was in a bar with a bunch of my friends. As I was making my way out, I heard something that still echoes in my head and, unfortunately, in the minds of much of the public.
>
> The female bar owner was dating a high-ranking officer of a local police department. As I was heading out the door, he spoke very loudly to his lady: 'Why would you let a guy like that come into this bar? You know he's the president of his club and he had to kill someone to get that position!'
>
> Now, I had many friends in there and they've all known me for half a lifetime. They knew the cop's assertion was preposterous. Someone in his position should know better, or at the very least, use his abilities to get the facts. That bar lost a lot of business that day; we, of course, never went back. The real crime that was exposed that day was found in the lies that this officer had learned so well.
>
> Believe it or not, in all my years in this lifestyle, I still haven't killed anyone.
>
> Or taken a drug.
>
> Or even smoked a cigarette.
>
> All my vices are wet ones!
>
> And *that* is the truth.

REACTION AND RESPONSE

"Cryptic symbols, rituals, rites and practices" have a way of rising to a neck-deep level in any group that prefers to be "exclusive." But in the biker world, the "cloak and dagger stuff" is often examined in a context of sensationalistic—and outdated—conjecture. Facts and fun are laid out like that corpse on a slab—not even a conscious part of the licking being dealt out.

CHAPTER 5:

WHEN PUPPETS BREED

SECRET NUMBERS AND SUPPORT CLUBS

INTERROGATING THE SUBJECT

Law enforcement says that support clubs are "farm teams" and "ducks."
The clubs themselves use the word "honor" to describe their backing
of the bigs. Who's right?

Me and my uncle are having a heated discussion on whether the real-life
Sons of Anarchy is a biker gang or a biker club. I say gang, and he says club.

—A comment from an online
"TV tips and news" site about *Sons of Anarchy*

During *SOA*'s first run, this Internet forum—one of many—boasted 12,199 members. That's a big chunk of people spending a big chunk of time threading together insightful and obviously well-thought-out comments about a television show and the one-percent lifestyle.

Membership numbers are important to motorcycle clubs, too, for a variety of reasons. But "real-life" clubs seldom, if ever, post those numbers. No user lists or membership rosters are publically issued, and it's considered improper protocol or, at the very least, an unhealthy question for an outsider to ask a patch-holder—especially a high-ranking officer—"So, *bro*, how many guys you got in this club now?"

No.

That's like shaking hands with your riding gloves on, initiating a heavy inter-club conversation with dark shades hiding your eyes, or lurking around with your hands in your pockets.

It's just not done.

It can get folks *agitated*.

But numbers mean a lot. They reflect strength. They reflect a *presence*. And strength and presence translate into "L and R"—love and respect. Respect being the lead word.

But the numbers don't necessarily have to be big in terms of mathematics; they have to be big in terms of commitment and dedication. Big in terms of having enough numbers to cover each member's back. This community can sense when clubs have numbers with that kind of fire—or not. This community has deep primal instincts when it comes to discerning the truth.

ACCEPTANCE INTO THE ELITE

The media recently reported that over seven thousand motorcycle clubs have cropped up around the world since the airing of the latest spate of television shows about this way of life. That probably can't be substantiated, but what *can* be substantiated is that at every Confederation of Clubs meeting, as well as many impromptu bar summits and sit-downs, hopeful new organizations express their desire for existence.

They express their respect to the power clubs in that region. They present the prototypes of their colors for consideration. They ask for acceptance into the elite. And they show some numbers—numbers that may or may not ultimately produce that MC magic of long-lived strength and presence. Time really is the biggest arbiter of that, even *if* probationary blessings from the already-established are bestowed. Time will always reveal whether the physical and mental mettle of a motorcycle club is up to the task of providing those very special kinds of numbers.

DRINKIN' ON DRAFT DAY

Sometimes those special numbers are recognized, assimilated, or even assembled as *support* clubs: the "special teams," in some ways, of the MC world. They are generally smaller clubs that, for a variety of reasons, have pledged backing and support for a bigger club. A club could be located in a specific area that has many chapters of a major, for example, so a natural common geographical ground is the bond.

There is also the independence/autonomy factor. Maybe a long-running smaller club wants to retain its patch and heritage but also express its agreement with the overall policies, practices, and even the image of a more prominent club—another reason for *support*. There are many more reasons, including just simple alliances.

And that's good enough.

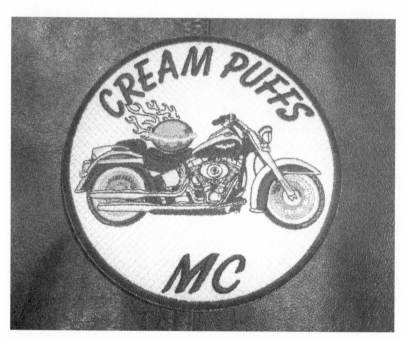

The authorities not-so-sweetly refer to round support patches as "cookies," but this particular MC patch may be a little more in line with that bite-sized brand. *Archives of Bill Hayes*

Alliances are a very human part of life. They're what make politics *politics*. Alliances fill sports stadiums and movie theaters. They form the perimeters for circles of close yet independent friends. They are the fuel for every high-blast reality show at the top of the ratings chart. Alliances define fans and friends of anything.

And there is always strength in numbers. It's another of those very human—and very comforting—parts of life.

But law enforcement likes to refer to MC support clubs as "farm teams," "puppet clubs," and "breeding grounds"—as if the majors get together on some kind of designated drink 'n' draft day and make their pick of new players to refill their crime pool. The authorities actually have sly slurs for the rookies: "mules," "conduits," "buffers," "servants," and even "ducks," who ostensibly carry out business so that the big boys can remain insulated from certain final scores if that *business* suffers some bad games.

> California may see an increase in the use of surrogate or "puppet" clubs. The larger clubs may implement the use of their support clubs to carry out their activities. These smaller clubs are becoming more violent in order to make a name for themselves and prove their worth to the appropriate club.
> —*Organized Crime in California*,
> Annual Report to the California Legislature,
> Office of the Attorney General, California Department of Justice, 2003

Or maybe they'll just help with events and projects, and enjoy the mutual brotherhood of like minds.

There's a concept.

CLAIMING THE COOKIE, CUTTING THE STRINGS

> 1% clubs will have several local support clubs in each state in which they have chapters. Investigators need to be aware which 1% clubs these smaller clubs support.
> —Texas Joint Crime Information Center, Information Bulletin, 2009

Well, that should be easy, because the same bulletin explained how supporters like "official hang-a-rounds" wear a round patch they call a "support cookie."

That represents some savory investigative scrutiny.

Yes, support clubs proudly wear the support patch—uh, "cookie"—of a more major club, but they are also often very vocal and straight up about their individuality. Statements on support clubs' websites and in other places make those sentiments clear with declarations like: "We are honored to support _____, but haven't been, refuse to be, and never will be anyone's 'bitch club'" and "We are proud and privileged to support _____. Our bond with them is strong and earned through years of living and riding side by side. We are a family of determined choice, not mere coincidence."

Those are emotions and declarations with wallop; as they should be. Words like that tend to cut the marionette-manacles that law enforcement has cinched up.

Authorities evidently don't get it that "ducks" in "breeding ground" seldom quack of honor and privilege.

They also don't get the common-sense dynamic that no entity, large or small, in power—especially in this lifestyle—wants to be aligned with or supported by anyone or anything perceived to be weak. Strong support is one thing; limp, mule-dumb subservience is something very, very different.

REACTION AND RESPONSE

The existence of support clubs is undisputed, but law enforcement has continually reduced them to lackey status. Statements from the clubs—both the supporters and the supported—indicate they are far above that level.

PART II

Chronicles of the Culture

CHAPTER 6:

ONE MORE
FOR THE ROAD
AT JOHNNY'S

THE HOLINESS OF HOLLISTER, THE SINS OF THE SCRIBES

INTERROGATING THE SUBJECT

Is anything new or different ever said by the media—or anyone else for that matter—when it comes to telling the story of Hollister '47?

> Now there were other motorcycles on the sidewalk. One of them hit a parked car at the edge of the walk. The rider standing astride his machine beat the window out of the car with his gloved fists.
>
> —Frank Rooney, "Cyclists' Raid"

Like Christmas and the chestnuts long roasting on that open fire, the story of Hollister, California, and the 1947 Gypsy Tour has been told "many times, many ways"—through books, magazines, film, and more. The city's history and alcohol-elevated earning of the title "the Birthplace of the American Biker" have made it a motorcycle Mecca.

A quick recap of Hollister's tumultuous timeline starts with the "riot" in 1947 during the AMA's golden-ruled Gypsy Tour, a happy-go-lucky Independence Day weekend of structured racing and good clean fun. Of course, that was all soiled and sullied forever by the nasty drunken rowdiness of bikerdom's bad seeds—the evil element that, according to legend, spawned the hideous demon called the "one-percenter"!

The media monster rose up from the downtown rubble! The *San Francisco Chronicle*, *Life* magazine, and photographer Barney Peterson unleashed unnerving photographs of marauding motorcyclists upon the straight world. Peterson's photos, of course, were rumored to have been a set-up of sensationalism—an accusation later proven to be true. Nevertheless, they launched a fear and panic that had no reverse gear.

Writers and film producers soon joined in the carnage. In January of 1951, *Harper's* magazine published Frank Rooney's Hollister-inspired short story, "Cyclists' Raid," and the ever-chilling specter of "a biker gang taking over a town" was given life. Two years later, in 1953, producer Stanley Kramer released his film *The Wild One*, and the beast was rampaging! Brando, Marvin, Johnny, Chino, leather jackets, skull back-patches, bad bikes, a doe-eyed babe with an outlaw crush—the world was changed forever!

A few years down the road, '60s flicks and rags were mauling the public with titles and headlines such as *Satan's Sadists*, *Motorpsycho!* and *Biker Orgy: Wild Roaring Sex Rides by the Devil Angels on Wheels*!

Hollister was truly the gateway drug for the media's mainlining of some very potent stimulation.

Then more serious writers, filmmakers, and historians began to look at the legacy of Hollister. They performed careful examinations and crafted the facts. Some were scholastically sterile; journals and theses abounded. All the eggheads realized and acknowledged Hollister's importance and how it has influenced all of biker and motorcycle club culture from the 1940s to present day.

But with few exceptions, so many bottom-lined with the same things repeated over and over. "Many times, many ways" gave way to monotony. Details of what happened became singular sound bites about the innocence of the area and the AMA's definition of one-percenter—Googling the term "sleepy little town of Hollister" yields 21,200,000 hits alone. Emotion and analysis became cold and tired summation rather than a walk in the warm wind of Hollister's streets, focusing on reflections of ghosts in store windows, seeking out the words of those who truly were a part of the *fun* and its aftermath, and sitting down for a night of drinking in Johnny's Bar.

GETTING WILD WITH WINO

"Wino Willie" Forkner was there in 1947, riding up to Hollister from Los Angeles. He was charismatic and woozily winsome. Myths, mysteries, and rumors have cited Wino as being the literal role model for Lee Marvin's character of "Chino" in *The Wild One*. And that makes perfect sense: Chino was much more loose and lovable than Brando's brooding Johnny.

The scribes always mention Forkner in their riot-reviews, but seldom are his own words and thoughts exhumed and examined. But in the late 1980s, *Easyriders*

The legendary, the iconic, the mythical Johnny's Bar. *Bill Hayes*

magazine began to release a series of "video magazines." With Dave Mann masterwork covers wrapped around big ol' clunky VHS tapes, an amazing latter-day history of this lifestyle—perhaps more by accident than on purpose—was preserved. Tucked away in a corner of the series' eighth volume is a rare interview with Wino.

His words added a lot of humanism to the myths, mysteries, and rumors of why Hollister—and this whole lifestyle—erupted in the first place. His booze-swilling saga of crashing a rules-and-regulation AMA event bares the emotions and attitudes that were in the collective soul of returning World War II veterans:

We all came back [from the war] with the same thing in mind: "Jesus, now we can kind of play and do hairy things and no one is shootin' at our ass." That made a hell of difference in life... When there's no bullets flying, by god, you can have a pretty good time.

[About a year before Hollister] they had the first AMA-sanctioned quarter-mile at El Cajon, California, and being the first race since the war, they didn't perform too good. Me and Blackie were up in the grandstand with the public, and the crowd's kind of hissin' and booin'... me and ol' Blackie suckin' on that bottle of booze and I said, "Jesus Christ, we could put on a better show than this!" So we staggered out to the parking lot, and the road went right down to the big gate they had at the back of the pits.

He said, "How the hell are we gonna get in there?"

I said, "You're gonna go right through that goddamned gate!"

He said, "Holy shit!"

I said, "All you gotta do is lay down on that goddamned tank and hang on. When you get close to the gate, you'll go through!"

So we took off going full-tilt, and I never looked up at that son of a bitch because I was intent on seeing where I'm going through those boards. And shit, the next thing I know, the boards are flying and I'm getting sideways, and when I get it straightened up I'm headed right down the straightaway!

Son of a bitch, I don't know how the hell that ever happened! So I just hooked it all on, I thought that bastard [Blackie] was right alongside of me. Shit, he just chicken-shitted out. He never even hit the goddamned gate! Just me by myself! Then, of course, the damned grandstand came alive. They just jumped up a-whooping and hollering! I made a lap around there and [an official] came out with the flag rack like he's gonna hit me over the head with it, so I do a little sashay toward the infield and he dropped it and ran.

I made another goddamned lap. How the hell I didn't fall down, I don't know. So he comes out with a chair the next lap around; I run him back into the infield. I think I made a fourth lap before I finally fell on my ass in the south turn and J. D. John comes running over and pulled the mag wires off this son-of-a-bitch, and I sat there like an asshole trying to crank it for fifteen or twenty minutes before I realized it ain't gonna run....

"THAT BASTARD'S DRUNK; HE NEEDS THE REST!"

But men and machines were back in full motion by the time the fuse was lit for Independence Day 1947. Wino Willie and his boys were ready for a "hardy party" as they made the three-hundred-mile putt up to Hollister on their vintage iron. Any thoughts of making history weren't even on the table—booze bottles were.

One of the main myths, mysteries, and rumors rolling in the detail-dust of Hollister's "riot" concerns whether or not a jailbreak was pulled off in the middle of the mess.

Wino was rough, tough, and raw, but he describes the notorious "breakout" with innocence and smiles, draining much of the rush from the bad-PR potions that were passed around again and again after that famous Fourth:

> We got [to Hollister] the day before the three-day event was supposed to start. Well, Jesus, we go through the whole ritual that night—drinkin' and raisin' hell—and the next night, Red Dahlgren got thrown in jail for being just plain drunk. And everybody's in the big hotel barroom there, and somebody said something about, "Let's go down and break Dahlgren out of jail." I didn't pay no attention to them, those assholes. There's about thirty, forty, fifty of them...they go down to that little two-bit jail and they're standing out front figuring out how they'll just bust the door down. And there's three cops standing in there, the local fuzz.
>
> My old lady comes to me and says, "You know, they're down there going to break Red out of jail!" I thought, *Jesus Christ, that's kind of stupid! That bastard's drunk; he needs the rest!* He's got a bunk to sleep on now instead of a car or the trailer. So I go runnin' down there and told them, "Hey, Red needs the rest; he'll be out in the morning. Let's get back to this hardy partying!"
>
> Well, those three cops in there, they're lookin' through the windows and they don't know what the hell I'm doin' there. I get all the crowd goin' back to the bar and, son-of-a-bitch, they come out of the door and grab *me* and put me in jail for inciting a riot!

How mistaken can you get?! But I stayed in jail, went to court in the morning, and I was still about half-stiff, but all my friends were in there, so, what the hell. It was a nice place to be!

It was quite a trip!"

A BABY–FACED BRANDO?

By the time Wino's "trip" was six years old, Rooney's raid and Kramer's reels had rolled through America. *The Wild One*, with a less-than-quiet debut in New York City, was especially inciting. Because of international postwar jitters that a "shocking 'Communist' movie glamorized an anti-social subculture in revolt," Stanley's show was immediately banned by the British Board of Film Censors and was not seen in England until 1968. Stateside, however, the black-and-white epic was not only seen but was ingested and digested into the fuel that ignited modern biker culture's image.

In 2008—fifty-five years after the movie's premier and fifty-five years of influence later—Sony Pictures released the *Stanley Kramer Film Collection* DVD box set. There, sandwiched in with remastered mega-classics like *Guess Who's Coming to Dinner* and *Ship of Fools* was *The Wild One*. The kicker was that the myths, mysteries, and rumors that haunted both the film and Hollister '47 were met head-on in some very "special features."

First, Stanley Kramer's widow, Karen, introduces the movie standing in front of a backdrop of bikes. She starts off with a little of the oh-here-we-go-again-about-the-riot stuff:

"This film is based on a true incident that happened on the Fourth of July in 1947, when four thousand motorcyclists descended on a sleepy little town in Northern California. The town was called Hollister. These motorcyclists supposedly terrorized the townspeople and ransacked the town. And when they'd had enough, after two days they simply roared off out of town."

There's that bottom line again; the simple summation that is seen so often. But Karen Kramer had more to say about what her husband saw in his film.

"This is the very first time in the history of this country when this sort of incident happened without real motivation or reason. Well, Stanley read about this in a magazine article and he couldn't understand it, because here we were in post–World War II—the most celebrated time in this country—when there was peace, there was plenty of money, plenty of jobs for people. There was hope, and on the surface everything seemed happy.

"Underneath all that was the unrest of the youth. There was a new breed of youth on the scene. Stanley used film very often to expose social issues…"

Youth?

Not bikers?

Not those hardened World War II vets, like Wino Willie, who were trying to reclaim their lives by finding refuge in their bikes and their brothers?

It was a more-than-compelling shift, but the reality is that the presence and power of the motorcycles made this movie magical in ways that apparently not even Kramer realized. Those machines made this movie about an edgy part of society that was about to be even more motivated by the fierce force of two wheels. Couple that with the fact that neither Marlon Brando nor Lee Marvin exactly exuded "new breed" baby-faced youth and juvenile delinquency. Both were nearly thirty years old when *The Wild One* was filmed; the real teen-like trials and tribulations of the day belonged to doomed pretty boys such as James Dean and Sal Mineo.

Brando and Marvin rebelled in the remote dusty streets of Wrightsville; Dean and Mineo struggled in the halls of Dawson High.

With all due respect to Stanley and Karen, *The Wild One* was ultimately *not* about kids.

SONY SCREENS THE SECRETS

Sony then became investigative reporters. In another special feature tacked on to the DVD—this one a half-hour long—they interviewed residents of Hollister who were there in '47. They interviewed bikers who were there. They interviewed the mayor. They interviewed historians. They tore apart the staged photographs of Barney Peterson. And, as with Wino's innocence and grins, they looked at that landmark weekend in terms of 1940s "trouble," not through the more violent and volatile prism of *now*. They turned back time and bottom lines in ways that few others have done. The myths, mysteries, and rumors of Hollister '47 were played out by many who were in the original line-up.

One of those interviewed was Charisse Tyson. She's way too young to have been there in '47, but she did become the owner of one of the event's most iconic relics, Johnny's Bar. Johnny's is where bikes were ridden in and out of the front door, setting the slippery stage for one of the lifestyle's most recognizable images. Nothing says "bar hoppin'" like actually riding the thing *through* the front door!

"On the weekend, we've got a lot of motorcycles cruising through," said Charisse. "Everybody wants to see Johnny's. People from France, Germany, all over the place. They've heard about Johnny's, so they want to come here. People just stand there all year long taking their picture in front of Marlon [a big cut-out of Brando in front of the bar]. It's really cool!"

Charisse, too, has penned some bottom lines about Hollister, but it's not what you might expect. *Born Again in a Biker Bar* is a book that blends alcoholism, Christianity, and co-dependency together in a place where those concepts were either ignored or clinically unclassified in '47. When Johnny's front-road of San Benito Street was being lined with the rubber of burn-outs and donuts, little was probably being said about self-help and spiritual salvation.

But for Charisse, it is now.

And that's Hollister.

It's a town and a story that has a lot more bottom lines for a lot more people than we often see and hear. Three crazy days birthed decades of media massaging, social speculation, brotherhood building, character studies, image-making, influence, redundancy, repentance, unending worldwide attention, one-percenters, and ultimately a title that is one hundred percent true.

REACTION AND RESPONSE

Yes. Even though many in the media have chosen to retell the basics over and over, for those who care to dig, plenty of fresh and fertile roots of history and their effects can still be discovered in and around "the sleepy little town" of Hollister.

CHAPTER 7:

GETTIN' CHUMMY WITH CHARLIE

THE STRAIGHT SATANS' STRANGE SOIRÉE WITH MANSON

INTERROGATING THE SUBJECT

Are you serious? Did Charles Manson really try to enlist
an outlaw motorcycle club as his personal bodyguard? And if so, who
were these guys? Does anyone know anything about them?

Corcoran, Calif,. November 18, 2014—Mass murderer Charles
Manson has gotten a license to marry a 26-year-old woman who
visits him in prison.

The Kings County marriage license, viewed Monday by The
Associated Press, was issued Nov. 7 for the 80-year-old Manson and
Afton Elaine Burton, who left her Midwestern home nine years ago
and moved to Corcoran, California—the site of the prison—to be
near Manson. She maintains several websites advocating Manson's
innocence...Burton, who goes by the name "Star," told the AP that
she and Manson will be married next month... "I love him," she
added. "I'm with him...."

"That's a bunch of garbage," Manson said in [a] December 2013
interview. "That's trash. We're playing that for public consumption."

California Department of Corrections spokeswoman
Terry Thornton confirmed to the AP that the license had been
transmitted to the prison...In most cases, she said, the department
of corrections approves of such weddings as "a tool of family
reunification and social development." But Manson is a unique case.

—The Associated Press

No kidding.

Very unique.

And in all these years, Manson's never lost his acrid ability to make headlines
or history.

The evil that Charles Manson engineered on the nights of August 8 and 9, 1969,
redefined mass murder and changed American culture—"pop" or otherwise—forever.
"Charlie" and his posse of freak-followers demonstrated to an impatient mainstream
and a growing silent majority that the "love generation" was the fraud they always knew
it was. That drugs do destroy. That dropping out of society to the depths that the '60s
eventually celebrated went well beyond being bohemian and eclectic. That burrowing
into such a low of an underground was a fall into filth and smothering from which there
was no escape.

Manson and his anti-society antics proved to be twisted living theater, presenting
the decade of the 1960s in excruciating exposition. Who he was and what he acted
out showed that the era had many more levels than love-ins, peace marches, political
confusion, and cool concerts.

"FUN, FUN, FUN," NOW THAT CHARLIE TOOK THE ROLLS-ROYCE AWAY!

Manson was a musician—of sorts—before he decided to orchestrate murder. His first attempt to hit the big time was to muscle into what was arguably the most poignant music scene in modern American history. This was completely counter to the happy harmony that had been supplying the soundtrack to the '60s. He had trouble rivaling work like *Sergeant Pepper* and *Are You Experienced?* with his album of tunes like "People Say I'm No Good," "Garbage Dump," and "Sick City."

His courting of the well-connected developed into a strange attachment and seemingly forced friendship with Beach Boy Dennis Wilson. Their relationship was the ultimate juxtaposition of pure pre-Beatles innocent fluff, later '60s rock that was getting heavier and heavier, and Manson's darkness. Having Charlie for a buddy led to Wilson enduring the entire Manson "family" squatting in his Sunset Boulevard mansion; his Rolls-Royce being commandeered for use by Manson's girls on garbage-food runs to supermarket dumpsters; his Mercedes being totaled by family member Clem; the disappearance of his clothes and gold records; and just an insane amount of money in general flushed down a sad, blood-sucking shitter.

"DONKEY DAN" DIDN'T LAUGH

Manson may have missed the mark when it came to music, but his focus on mass manipulation and other assorted desires to change the world was Buck-knife sharp. With that kind of big work ahead, Charlie saw a potential benefit to adding bikers to his ensemble.

Now, bikers of that day may have looked like hippies; they may have taken drugs like hippies and listened to rock 'n' roll like hippies.

But they weren't hippies.

Peace, love, flowers-in-your-hair, and dainty dancing drifts to Donovan songs weren't the things that got bikers off. They needed bigger and harder kicks than that, and Charlie knew it. And like any aspiring leader and violent visionary, he also knew he needed a loyal "army" to be his bodyguards and help accomplish his goals—an army that wasn't afraid to fight. Sure, he eventually convinced his family minions to murder, but he wanted to be surrounded by the constant protection of an ever-ready-for-trouble force.

Bikers were perfectly cast for the role.

Finally evicted from Dennis Wilson's digs on Sunset, the Manson family was now living at the Spahn Ranch in Los Angeles's San Fernando Valley. But Charlie got around. About thirty miles from Spahn, over the Sepulveda grade, was the beach town of Venice. With its odd canals and an overall eclectic atmosphere, Venice was the comfortable stomping (sometimes literally) grounds of many bikers and motorcycle clubs.

It was there that Manson first ran into the Straight Satans MC.

According to statements made by former family member seventeen-year-old Kitty Lutesinger during the later murder trial, that's when Charlie tried to "enlist" the club. But according to Kitty, most of the club just laughed at Manson.

Most, but not all.

Straight Satans Treasurer Daniel DeCarlo decided to hang around. The family's sex and drugs held a certain appeal for "Donkey Dan."

DeCarlo ended up being pivotal in the Manson murder trial. He and prosecutor Vincent Bugliosi wound up spending a lot of quality time together:

> I interviewed Danny numerous times, one session lasting nine hours, obtaining considerable information that hadn't come out in previous interviews. Each time I picked up a few more examples of Manson's domination. . . . Although DeCarlo was extremely reluctant to testify, [LaBianca case detective] Sergeant Gutierrez and I eventually persuaded him that it was in his own best interests to do so.
> —Vincent Bugliosi, *Helter Skelter*

And while the rest of the Straight Satans may have chuckled at the just-over-five-foot crazy Charlie, ultimately they didn't completely shun the fun at Spahn, either. Joining his "army" was rejected, but they fell into an ongoing up-and-down association with Manson and the family that would immortalize the club.

A HISTORY FROM HELL

The Straight Satans were a small group swirling within Southern California's wide world of growing MCs that were making big names and a long-lasting legacy for themselves. Chances are that the Straight Satans would have faded into the background colors of the more well-known and powerful clubs, but because of Manson they became—like Charlie himself—truly unique.

But it has taken a while for every fine detail of the legend to be uncovered.

Other than the news reports during the Tate-LaBianca murder trial and the staid exposure the club received in the late Vincent Bugliosi's book *Helter Skelter*, the Straight Satans have remained steeped in myths, mysteries, and rumors. Their eerie and everlasting connection to events that killed an entire era floated randomly around for years and years, like the muck on what was left of Venice's canals.

Until a young man named Bo Bushnell became interested.

For years he has been digging up forgotten—and sometimes forbidden—treasure that gleams with blinding beams, illuminating even the most lost of lore in the biker culture.

He is the ultimate seeker of the sacred.

THE IMPORTANCE AND VALUE OF "OUTLAW PHOTOGRAPHY"

Bo's story of how one thing led to an archival other is like following the Xs on a tattered treasure map. In this case, each path leads to an even bigger bounty than the last.

"I knew the folklore of the Straight Satans from the Manson murders," Bo began, "having read *Helter Skelter* when I was younger. I also knew about collectors of rare photos and other memorabilia of historical occurrences, especially dealing with the motorcycle culture. I was dabbling in that, when in April of 2013 I received an e-mail from a guy who said his mom had passed away and he had inherited the Straight Satans scrapbook.

"I didn't believe him. I asked him for some sample photos, but he said he would never digitize them. This treasure dig was winding up as an empty hole.

"Then I went to this show called 'Printed Matter' at the Museum of Contemporary Art in Los Angeles. A vendor there had three hundred seventy-five Crips photos from the '80s. I made a deal with the guy for like $2,500. 'Just let me finish scanning them and archiving them,' he told me. 'Give me a month and they're yours.'

"A month and a half later, I hadn't heard back from him," Bo lamented. "Another empty pit?"

His answer would come in an awkward place at an awkward time.

"I'm sitting on the toilet one morning and a friend sends me a link to a news article: '400 Crips photos sell for $45,000 at the Paris Photo Los Angeles exhibition.'

"I went nuts. Then I remembered that Straight Satans album. I kept thinking that outlaw photography of any sort is important. There's value to it. And it's not just about money.

"I found that guy's e-mail and asked if the album was still available. His answer was yes; and this time he sent me some digital images. I was blown away!

"I spent a month negotiating with him and got it, and that opened up a very special Pandora's Box."

ONE SATAN LEADS TO ANOTHER

Armed with an information arsenal, Bo went to work.

"I spent a month dissecting the album. I put together a list of every name I could find in it and I made nearly two thousand phone calls, literally.

"Then I found 'Droopy,' a.k.a. 'Slave Rick.' He was the first truly club-involved person I finally made contact with. And he gave me enough information to find other people. And each person led me to the next person. Droopy led me to Howard, an original member of one of Venice's most major MCs. He had been around the Straight Satans and his history went back to the '50s and very early '60s. It was amazing to hear his stories," Bo explained.

And he obviously listened well.

"Besides leading me to more Straight Satans, his lore opened up all of the Southern California bike culture to me. And that's the coolest thing. Everybody has the conception that most history came out of Oakland and 'Frisco. So much did happen up north, but so little information is out there about the SoCal scene in the '60s.

"The famous-infamous November '65 *Saturday Evening Post* article was written here, for example; but unfortunately, that was so long ago that people my age or even a little older don't even know what *The Saturday Evening Post* is or was, let alone how important that article was.

"That article was written by a man named Bill Murray. Well, I have the minutes to the Straight Satans' meetings from 1960 to '61, and they mention a visitor named Bill Murray. It has to be the same guy.

"This guy got around and wrote about what he saw.

"This is history."

RESURRECTING—AND RESPECTING—THE PAST

And Bo Bushnell is so right about that. The history that he was about to chronicle was priceless; at least to those in the lifestyle—*truly* in the lifestyle. Those who understand what all of this was—and is.

"That one photo album dominoed," Bo continued. "It allowed me to find out so much. The Straight Satans members alive today have no photos; it's the families of deceased members who have the archives. 'Listen,' I went to them and said, 'I have this, and this should be with this....Let's get it all in one place.'

"They were all cooperative and wanted to see the history of this club presented with the prominence it deserves. What I have acquired has to be the largest single archive of a true one-percenter club from '60s SoCal in existence.

"When I say 'one percent,' I mean the original one percent coalition of just four clubs.

"And, really, what I have been building up in the way of historical relics—way beyond the Straight Satans—isn't exclusively MC culture, it's motorcycle culture, period.

"We can all look back and see the way the choppers were built and who the important pioneer builders were. Everybody knows who Ed 'Big Daddy' Roth was, but it's crazy to find out about people who should be as famous as Roth but aren't. Like Dean Lanza. Back in the '60s and '70s he was known as 'The Dean' of custom bike painting in Los Angeles. I know a young guy who's restored four Dean Lanza bikes, in an effort to rebuild the name and brand image of Lanza and why he was so important.

"We can't forget about 'C. B. Clausen on Slauson,' either. With his MC Supply, the shop of shops, he had the heart and soul of motorcycle parts in Los Angeles.

"And then there's Bob George, the engine builder who to this day has a world record at Bonneville [Salt Flats] after designing and building the record-setting double-engine, nitro-burning, Shovelhead-powered Jammer Liner. But he also invented the

The arrest of Charles Manson and his accomplices for a series of mass murders in 1969 provided a horrific coda to the decade of sex, drugs, and rock and roll. *Photo by ullstein bild via Getty Images*

Charles Manson was arrested at the Barker Ranch in Death Valley, shown here. To convince the elderly woman who owned the ranch to let him and his "family" hide out there, Manson gave the woman a Beach Boys gold record that had been given to him by one-time friend Dennis Wilson. © *william girard girard/Alamy Stock Photo*

water-cooled engine for motorcycles. He was the first to run oil through the frame of a bike. At one point he needed money so badly that he got a loan from a friend, who, as collateral, got to hang onto Bob's bike—a bike he showed everybody, resulting in Bob's loss of a patent on the process. Bob George spent everything he had trying to get his invention back, but in the end he lost everything. He wound up living in a trailer in Hemet."

"O SOLE MIO" IN THE WILD WEST

And the dominoes continued to fall—uphill, in a positive direction. Biker history was opening up into more social history, beyond even Manson. But it was all tied so tightly together.

"All of this exploration opened up the world of Venice to me," said Bo, "the last of the wild, wild West. It was like the Pirates of the Caribbean on acid.

"The town was originally called 'Venice of America,' but the canals that were supposed to be the center of the Euro-ambience fell into a nasty neglect. So did the residents.

"The characters I discovered in that place and time—both in and out of the Straight Satans—are larger than life. You can't make them up. Today, Venice's circus-like Ocean Front Walk is Southern California's premier freak show. That's how all of Venice was back then—an entire city made up of the stars of a crazed carnival. And those freaks weren't there to entertain tourists like they are today; they were the weirdos of the world in the perfect place for them—'Where the debris meets the sea.' Where city and county abandonment allowed the whole place to become, by the 1950s, the 'Slum by the Sea.'

"The home-sweet-home of the Straight Satans."

JUST A BUNCH OF CRAZY CUT-UPS

But Manson left a permanent—and poisonous—mark on everyone he touched. Becoming chums with Charlie didn't exactly elevate the SSMC's membership ranks.

"After the Manson trial, things remained dicey for the club," Bo explained, revealing more and more details from his investigations and track-downs. "A Straight Satan named Bobby stabbed a guy seventy-nine times because he had a bogus club tattoo. The guy was at a bar bragging that he was a member.

"He wasn't."

That's never a good situation.

"That guy didn't know that real club members were in the bar and, yes, they overheard him. They 'invited' him to come down to the canals where Bobby gutted him; but only after the tattoo was sliced off of him.

"Bobby only spent a year and a half in jail for the filleting, but the heat got so bad that no one was able to fly colors in Venice.

"The Straight Satans had originated up the road in Santa Monica and shortly thereafter had opened a San Fernando Valley chapter—the SFV. Eventually they moved everything to Venice. After the crackdown, they transferred all operations to nearby Westchester and Inglewood."

It was a fateful foreshadowing. Today, Inglewood is high on lists of cities most terrorized by urban street gangs.

THE GREATEST INSURANCE POLICY

Bobby's little cut-up act aside, the Manson connection may not have expanded the club, but neither did it single-handedly bring about its end—it did, of course, have a weighty effect.

"The club had about thirty-five members at the time of Manson," Bo calculates, "but a split in the ranks did occur because of Danny DeCarlo. Donkey Dan had his own clique within the club. But the other side didn't like him because his testifying at the Manson trial gave them all 'snitch jackets' in the eyes of the rest of the community, including other one-percenters.

"The greatest insurance policy for continued breathing is continued silence.

"Half the club left. Of the half that stayed, three of the main members died back to back to back within a couple months of each other. Then a group of seventeen or eighteen local bikers were arrested for raping a fifteen-year-old. The party-pack included Straight Satans and other members of major clubs."

It was bad timing. In the gory glow of his post-Manson fame, prosecutor Vincent Bugliosi was running for Los Angeles County District Attorney. One of his main political pushes was that he was going to 'rid California of the one percent motorcycle clubs. They're destroying our communities.'

"That rape was a ready-made example of that 'destruction,'" agreed Bo, "and provided perfect campaign-slogan fodder. But the entire situation turned out to be a lose-lose—Bugliosi came up short in the election and the bikers involved in the attack each spent six to twelve years in jail.

"By 1973 only four members of the Straight Satans remained and they agreed to stop wearing their colors."

But that is not the end of the Straight Satans. Thanks to Bo Bushnell, at least the haunting history of this mythic club—and the characters who wore its patch—has many more chapters to be revealed.

REACTION AND RESPONSE

Manson absolutely did try to enlist the Straight Satans MC to be his "army." Although they declined Manson's pitch, the club still became integral in the Family. Even so, they have remained fairly obscure for decades. Luckily, they left behind a curious treasure chest of archives, now preserved by "the ultimate seeker of the sacred," Bo Bushnell.

CHAPTER 8:

COSTUME COPIES TO CUT-COLLECTING

MASKING AND MOCKING THE MONSTER

INTERROGATING THE SUBJECT

"So, you don't allow three-piece patches here, but—and let me get this straight—
I can buy and wear one of your t-shirts that's designed to *look like*
a three-piece patch?" Pretend colors, phony cuts on eBay, *real* cuts
on the black market, real cuts banned everywhere—what the hell's up with all this?

Dear Sir:

It has come to our attention that a new sign has been posted on the beach which says that no dogs will be allowed there-on. Therefore I am writing to protest this policy.

Very Sincerely Yours,

[Snoopy]

—Snoopy's letter to the editor, *Snoopy Come Home*

Watching in horror at 1972's *Snoopy, Come Home*, America cringed as its favorite lovable beagle was eighty-sixed from place after place, reeling under the painfully ostracizing "No Dogs Allowed" signs.

Even the gentle, feather-fluffed Woodstock felt the pangs of discrimination during the tense and tearful eighty-minute TV show.

But the sting of segregation has cut through more than just cartoons. Signs prohibiting certain people from certain places were common well into the 1960s, until legal canons and common sense finally became a bit calmer and cooler. Freedom regained some of its constitutional importance and has lasted and grown within ethnicities, genders, ages, religions, and virtually every social class.

With one exception.

> The Golden Nugget Casino-Hotel hereby adopts and enforces the following No Colors Policy: No person, while on the premises of the Golden Nugget Casino-Hotel, shall exhibit, or make visible to the naked eye, on his person, apparel, accessories, vehicles, or accoutrements any emblem, decal, insignia, badge, kerchief, or sign that suggests, states, displays, endorses, supports, or promotes any affiliation with, association with, sympathy for, support for, membership in, or endorsement of any motorcycle club, gang, association, or organization.
>
> —Sign posted at the Golden Nugget Casino-Hotel, Las Vegas

Damn, that's quite the airtight list! The only loophole might be in the "naked eye" part. Every garment, color, and tattoo is covered, but some microscopic "support" ink on the inside of your belly-button skin fold just might slip by. Then again, don't bank on it.

The Golden Nugget chain obviously wants nothing to do with motorcycle clubs on any level, and they're not alone. Anyone who even casually frequents bars, biker events, or Joe-Public places such as bowling alleys, county fairs, swap meets, amusement parks, and theme parks has seen the postings.

Some, though, are more interesting than others.

LEATHER, HORSEFLESH, AND RUGRATS AT RISK

Another large casino, this one in the heart of Palm Springs, displayed a big sign at its main entrance during the annual fall run at the desert oasis. It was a weird and nowhere near as inclusive spin on the Golden Nugget's screed. The posting proclaimed, "No One Is Allowed in the Casino Wearing Leather."

Hmm...now, does that include shoes and belts on businessmen and other "citizens"? Little old blue-hairs carrying purses? Obviously, that hot-spot in Palm Springs was trying to keep cut-wearing bikers and club members from disrupting their profitable pits, but along with poor legal writing, they missed something else: one of the major MCs in the area that was attending the event in large numbers does not wear leather cuts; they universally wear denim. As the weekend rolled on, that sign must have generated some lively debates.

Even the famed horse-racing venue, Santa Anita Park—established in Arcadia, California, in 1934 and considered by equine insiders to be "the world's most beautiful race track"—now has a version of the sign at its turnstiles. The sport of kings isn't generally thought of as a major attraction for packs of scooter tramps, but the big-bet boys aren't gambling on the possibility that some just might show up.

Increasingly, even Harley dealers have joined in the fence-building. Flyers for free-hot-dogs-and-soft-drinks-fun-and-live-band promos often have a little restriction inserted down at the bottom. In the interest of marketing and customer relations, however, they usually try to soften the blow with something like, "This is a family event, so we are asking your cooperation in observing our no-colors policy. Thank you!"

Of course, there's a back-door implication here that motorcycle club members have no families, no children, and are liable to have some sort of toxic effect on those who do.

BUSINESS VS. BIKERS

In truth, none of this is a surprise.

And this, like so many things in modern industrialized society, is about business.

Waves of paranoia that rippled out from years of bad press and well-publicized downers such as the shootings in Sturgis 1990, Laughlin 2002, Reno 2011, and Waco 2015 have panicked proprietors and promoters. But the insane amounts of money that bikers spend on their machines and merrymaking has a way of tempering that panic. Like the Harley dealers, business owners and event producers have wrestled with what they see as dollars-versus-danger. It must be morally uncomfortable to be in the hard-to-balance commercial position of trying to cultivate the good, wholesome, and clean sector of biker business while attempting to as-diplomatically-and-tactfully-as-possible shun those nasty outlaw-outcasts.

Echoes of the AMA's still-sacred 1947 sermon about the ninety-nine percent versus the one percent remain loud and clear.

But when it comes to the fractures between business and club members (or even those perceived to be the lifestyle's most serious and hardcore), signs and shut doors are not where myths, mysteries, and rumors are the strangest. Four murky questions in particular could use some clear answers:

Have bikers done anything to fight back?

How do some bars, restaurants, and events have the double-standard balls to exclude real patches while hawking their own lookalike merchandise?

How do overseas pirates get away with selling copy MC merchandise, and how dangerous is it?

Does an underground collector's market for stolen colors actually exist?

Runs and bars love the three-piece-patch look on their merchandise, but the real deal walking in? Not so much. *Jennifer Thomas*

LITIGATION AND LEANING

When bikers are pushed, they push back harder. As the you're-not-welcome-here signs increased, so did serious court battles and protests. Throughout the early 2000s, major MCs initiated lawsuits against many venues that exercised "no colors" policies. Oddly enough, county fairs have been among the venues most often entangled in MC discrimination proceedings (even though their most heinous crime against humanity might just be the deep frying of everything from Oreos to pickles).

A long-running old-school-style motorcycle swap meet billed as "the largest monthly gathering of riders in the USA" also became a target. Promoters suddenly decided to adopt a no colors policy; the result was a large, peaceful, cohesive, inter-club protest and boycott that led to a reversal of the rule.

Similar demonstrations against establishments and events have occurred nationwide, from Arizona to Michigan to Florida, and points in between.

The litigation and leaning has proven to be successful in many cases, but certainly not all. The big-market bars, especially, are holding their ground. *And* they are adding arrogant insult to annoying injury with some of their logo-laced threads.

PEEKING IN THE WINDOW OF A MINSTREL SHOW

Patches and clubs are seductive, and seduction is one of those factors that can translate into monetary success. The money-minds at many of the big-run mega-bars decided that keeping *real* patches at a safe distance while cashing in on their appeal was the happy merchandising medium.

It's a contradictory campaign that makes for quite a scene at the giant gin-joints in the middle of "bike weeks" everywhere.

> I just had to stop and take it all in for a minute or two. Trying to understand. I'd ridden into this big-ass parking lot of bikes, squeezed into a parking place, walked up to the door only to see that fucking sign. *Okay*, I thought, *you don't want my money; I don't need your eight-dollar beers.* But the truth was that they genuinely didn't need me. And they definitely didn't want me. There were wall-to-wall people in there, and a lot of them were wearing these run shirts—even some with that damn bar's name on them—that looked like soft colors. I felt like a black guy peeking in the window of an old-time minstrel show; a whole bunch of folks having fun pretending to be something they're not. Ain't that some shit?
> —Unnamed patch-holder outside one of the super-saloons,
> Sturgis, 2010

But it could be worse: innocent ignorance in other wardrobe choices could cause a person some very unwanted grief.

"BUY IT NOW OR BEST OFFER!"

Clubs are very careful in designing, producing, and selling their merchandise.

There are rules.

For example, the word "support" is very important in marketing anything to non-members, and generally, the actual name of the club is not used—certain euphemisms make it well understood just who the wearer's home team is. Another rigid rule is that soft colors (full representations of a club's patch on t-shirts, sweatshirts, etc.) are for members only, and obviously they are never, ever sold on the open market through networks such as eBay.

Well, almost never.

While eBay and other sources do a good job of policing items for sale in regards to trademark infringements, copyright violations, and other sneakiness, they can't do a *perfect* job. Occasionally, you will see them: shirts, watches, belt buckles, all kinds of things with full knock-off images of major MC's patches. Pirated copies with an item origin point usually listed as someplace in Asia—elusive thieves, almost impossible to find, and even harder to sue.

It's frightening on a couple of levels.

The trademark-copyright issues aside, the idea of some clueless kid—or adult—buying soft colors of a well-known MC and then wearing them in certain areas or running into actual members of that club is a bad one.

Luckily, the item listings don't stay up long; this kind of nervy news spreads quickly. Some clubs actually have "trademark officers" who comb selling sites, searching for this kind of fraud. But the pirates often set up other sites apart from the eBay types, short-lived stand-alone sites that are closed down as soon as harassment and threats heat up. Then they simply launch another one, attempting to attract buyers before they attract the rightful owners of the images. And through all the deception and disrespect, their counterfeit contraband continues to sell—and endanger the naïve and thick.

But there's a different kind of buyer out there that's interested in motorcycle-club-related items, and this buyer is anything but naïve. He knows what he wants and has plenty of money to get it.

BRIBES, PAYOFFS, AND PERSUASION

Secret collectors—and plunderers—of underground anything are, by definition, mythic and mysterious.

It's like stealing history.

Art and cultural property crime—which includes theft, fraud, looting, and trafficking across state and international lines—is a looming criminal enterprise with estimated losses in the billions of dollars annually.
—FBI report, 2015

To a very specialized group of shadow-connoisseurs, authentic patched cuts from heavyweight clubs are considered both "art" *and* "cultural." And valuable—both for their apparently arousing collector status, and for their profitability in sales and swaps.

Money talks, and these aficionados are delighted to part with it in the way of bribes, payoffs, and other forms of persuasion that can convince someone with access—oh, say, an individual in a law enforcement evidence room as a wild example—to throw some cuts their way.

Other sources unfortunately exist as well, and they all should be concerned. Discovery by police is one thing; club retaliation for such disrespect is something else. But maybe the danger element is part of that arousal. It's clear that these collectors are not the kinds of people who could ever actually *wear* a cut or be a part of the brotherhood that it represents. Just *having* them is stimulation enough; like porn hoarders who, for various reasons, have to live a life of flaccid fantasy over real flesh.

> I've seen these guys operate. I've seen them give big money to connections who give them the goods. I've seen them trade among themselves, bringing out stacks of cuts, going through them like old time trappers would go through pelts. I've seen them nearly drool when they come to the big names.
>
> —Associate of a cut-collector who prefers to remain anonymous

At least nobody ever skinned Snoopy and Woodstock, selling their hides to the highest bidders.

REACTION AND RESPONSE

What the hell's up is that unethical and brazen business practices have cashed in—and crashed in—on the biker brotherhood. While feared and frozen out of so much of society, the MC image is a known moneymaker and a magnet for oily opportunists.

PART III

Countries in Chaos

CHAPTER 9:

THE THUNDER (AND BLUNDERS) DOWN UNDER

BIKIES, TRIBES, AND TRIBUNAL TRIBULATIONS

INTERROGATING THE SUBJECT

What in God's name are Australia's "Vicious Lawless Association Disestablishment (VLAD) laws" all about? And they're going to have a bikie-only prison?!

Okay, I know it's hard for those who live in the hemisphere where the toilet flushes the *right* way (another myth for another time!) to feel comfortable referring to the motorcycle culture as "bikies." But, hell, that's how they do it "Down Under." Australia also has eucalyptus-euphoric bears, wombats, dingoes, droning didgeridoos, endless extreme-deserts, and AC/DC.

There's a proud uniqueness on and around the twenty-sixth parallel south.

And when it comes to biker—sorry, mate; I mean *bikie*—evolution, a tsunami's-worth of history floods the island-continent and its far-Pacific neighbor, New Zealand.

The first international chapter of a major US MC began riding in New Zealand way back in 1966. Since then, it's been throttle-on. Well over forty powerful clubs have been established in Australia and New Zealand, two regions with a combined population of around twenty-nine million (just a couple million more than the state of Texas). Along with chapters of American clubs, indigenous MCs have grown, some with heavy Māori and Pacific Islander heritages.

And yes, there have been "incidents" that have produced a few negatives. On September 2, 1984, a shoot-out between clubs—the so-called "Milperra Massacre," in a suburb of Sydney—left seven people dead and twenty-eight injured. That fatal Father's Day in Australia made some horrific history: the "massacre" is universally recognized as one of the most infamous of all club battles.

And Sydney never did cool off in terms of its edginess.

BROTHERS AND BUNYIPS

Twenty-four years later, in 2008, thirteen bikie-related shootings blasted through the capital city in the space of two weeks. A year after that, a very public fatal clash between clubs touched down at the Sydney Airport; with plenty of media around to cover it all.

Australian authors such as Caesar Campbell, Adam Shand, Duncan McNab, Felicity Zeiher, Ron Stephenson, and the controversy-certain Arthur Veno have churned out plenty of books about Aussie and Kiwi clubs and calamities.

In 1986, the writing team of Lindsay Simpson and Sandra Harvey produced *Brothers in Arms*, the landmark work about Milperra, and in 2012, the book-based miniseries *Bikie Wars: Brothers in Arms* aired on Australia's Network Ten.

As in the US, the commonwealth's media has had a long love-hate affair with their outlaws. The government's feelings in regards to these matters, however, are much more "bloody-minded"; the "love" part is about as common as a fantasy-fanged bunyip in the Outback.

A RECIPE FOR TYRANNY

And this is where the myths, mysteries, and rumors in the Australian–New Zealand bikie scene now have the strength and push of a Mallee bull—but none of it is about those who ride. Club growth, history, and incident-infamy is secondary; it's the lawmakers, law enforcement, and politicians who create the headlines.

And the wars.

> American author and screenwriter David Simon has described
> Queensland's anti-bikie laws as a "recipe for tyranny" in a stinging
> criticism of the state's hardline new legislation designed to rid the
> area of outlaw motorcycle gangs.
> — Oliver Laughland, *The Guardian*, media blog, November 1, 2013

Once the rules, regulations, and restraints were locked on, each additional one has thickened the chains. In a quick-fix move eerily similar to the California legislature's reaction to the Black Panther Party's 1967 demonstrations at the state capitol, the Milperra aftermath led to tighter gun laws. One of the clubs involved in the shootings was well-known for openly—and lawfully—carrying shotguns, just as the Panthers did.

But certainly, all of *that* had to stop.

California countered the BPP's aggressiveness by rapidly passing a chokehold legislation called the Mulford Act; similarly, the state of New South Wales amended an older law, the New South Wales Firearms and Dangerous Weapons Act 1973, radically changing registered owners' rights to carry firearms in public to now requiring "a good reason for the issue of a [firearm] licence."

And who do you think gets to define that "good reason"?

As the years went "flat chat," other laws and debates blew through Australia's states and territories that would/could affect the club culture and its very existence; governmental gales such as the Drugs Misuse Act 1986, the Weapons Act 1990, the Criminal Proceeds Confiscation Act 2002, and the Corrective Services Act 2006 swept in.

South Australia's Statutes Amendment (Anti-Fortification) Act 2003 was especially destructive, designed "to prevent the construction of outlaw motorcycle gang headquarters in South Australia and also to allow police to demolish the existing fortifications when they are excessive."

And again, who do you think gets to define "excessive"?

In May 2008, the state of South Australia struck again, passing the Serious and Organised Crime (Control) Act 2008. That little cyclone of codes enhanced previous "anti-gathering" statutes: "the old law of consorting will be replaced with a new law of criminal association that prohibits telephone calls as well as meetings in the flesh."

It's difficult to be in a club together when you can't *be* together or even *talk* together.

Higher bail and longer jail sentences for bikies brought even harsher hell to the hail. The ingredients in the recipe for tyranny were rotting with bitterness; the lingering bad taste was getting worse.

Much worse.

TAKE A SQUIZZ AT *THIS* LAW!

On October 16, 2013, the Parliament of Queensland enacted the Vicious Lawless Association Disestablishment Act 2013—VLAD.

The supercell had hit.

For all of the legalese and wonkiness that entwine a major law like this, a few easy-to-navigate surges are felt in the storm.

One is that the law allows "the government, rather than the courts, to declare certain organisations 'criminal.'"

That in itself makes any sort of due process "not the full quid."

Then comes further non-association clampdowns: "The Act applies to legal organisations and 'any other group of 3 or more persons by whatever name called, whether associated formally or informally and whether the group is legal or illegal.'"

And once an organization is declared criminal, that's when the social solitary-confinement really begins.

VLAD THE IMPALER

"The new laws," said South Australia State Attorney General John Rau in 2015, "would also make it an offence for members of a criminal organisation to recruit anyone to become part of a criminal organisation, enter a licensed venue wearing or carrying a prohibited item such as colours (patches) or clothing identifying a criminal gang, enter a place or event that has been banned by serious and organised crime regulations."

In November 2014, VLAD survived a High Court challenge in Queensland. There have been many, but this latest had national implications—like a possible continent-wide whirlwind of "extra powers for Queensland's Crime and Corruption Commission," raising up that very special bikie-only prison at Woodford, north of Brisbane; mandatory sentences of fifteen years for serious crimes committed as part of gang activity, *on top of* the normal penalty; club office-bearers sentenced to an additional ten years in jail, with parole only granted if the offender cooperates with police (i.e., forced snitchery); convicted bikies subjected to strict drug tests and searches in prison; bikie criminals in other state prisons transferred to Woodford; a "licensing regime for tattoo parlours and artists, banning bikie gang members"; and the ultimate show of we-have-the-power: "motorcycles to be crushed as punishment for certain crimes."

Bikers in the US may have to deal with everything from RICO (the Racketeer Influenced and Corrupt Organizations Act of 1970) to I'm-gonna-stick-this-decibel-meter-up-your-exhaust-pipe noise ordinances and aftermarket equipment assaults, but actual government sanctioned prisons for bikers only?!

Laws against even calling a club brother on the phone?

Tattoo parlors—sorry, *parlours*—limited to sook-ish flash like Hello Kitty tramp stamps?

And watching your beloved scoot fork-lifted into a metal-crusher after hearing a "Guilty!" verdict?

"Crikey, mate!"

It seems like those "whacker" bikies are at the top of all Down Under's ills!

But that may not be the case.

"IT'S NO GOOD BLAMING THE BIKIES"

Campbell Newman, the Premier of Queensland until February 2015, said, "These criminals [bikies] seem to have lost touch with reality and we are going to reclaim the streets."

Well, reclaimed streets or not, the leading cause of death for Australians ages fifteen to forty-four—the prime-time life—is suicide. That mathematically boils down to almost seven per day. Bikie violence isn't even close to being in the same league with those numbers. The continent also struggles with increases in racial violence between various factions, as well as sexual assaults among and upon its citizenry.

Narcotics take a tortuous toll as well. The *Guardian* has reported that "Australia has one of the world's most serious drug problems, according to a major international study on the health burden caused by amphetamines, cocaine, cannabis, and opioids." And it's a problem not necessarily generated by the bikies, claims Aussie radio personality Tom Elliott.

In March 2015, Elliott told his listeners, "It's no good blaming the bikies. The bikies wouldn't be supplying the drugs if we didn't want to buy them. And when I say we, I mean many, many people in our community"—a community with quite a legacy of its own.

We all know that in the seventeen- and eighteen-hundreds, England began settling Australia as a penal colony. Fine, things are "pretty spiffy" now. But even then, nothing in that history hints at prisoner segregation by lifestyle-type or crime category—or the government's wanton punitive destruction of their personal property.

It appears that in the land where toilets are rumored to flush backwards, the system has been badly overloaded and things are genuinely starting to stink.

REACTION AND RESPONSE

Australia's Vicious Lawless Association Disestablishment (VLAD) laws are an unapologetic attempt to rid the region of motorcycle clubs. Totally. Completely. Pure and simple. Australia has plenty of other considerations when it comes to crime control, but the targets bikies wear on their backs are so big and easy to aim at. And as the government has become a statute-slinging sharpshooter, mysteries, myths, rumors, and law enactments keep pointing toward a very draconian answer to the question of whether MCs will exist Down Under in the future at all.

CHAPTER 10:

WHAT WOULD MAO DO?

A THREE-PIECE CULTURAL REVOLUTION?!

INTERROGATING THE SUBJECT

No way! An American started—and has grown—a three-piece patch MC in the People's Republic of China. How does that fly?

Mao may be right. For example, about having the "genuine knowledge" of what it's like to not only become a brother in a three-piece-patch, one-percent-diamond-wearing motorcycle club, but to start one.

In the People's Republic of China.

As a Birmingham, Alabama–born white guy.

All of that adds up to a very deep wok's worth of "direct experience."

In 2009, American Clay Jones established the Long March MC in a serious land, stir-fried in Red-hot myths, mysteries, and rumors.

And imposing strength.

It's safe to say that to most Westerners, the China giant is more about a socio-political and industrial power-focus than an easy environment of fun bar hops and casual runs out to the Great Wall on scoots. But are both of those images now entwined along the PRC landscape?

Chairman Mao had another good point when he said: "If you want to know the theory and methods of revolution, you must take part in revolution." More than likely, bikes and brothers weren't foremost on his mind, but, hey, if the silk slipper fits . . .

The biker lifestyle has always been one of revolution, and Clay Jones and his Long March MC are definitely taking part—in a land where theory and methods can be tricky.

"LOOK INTO MY EYES!"

Wherever you live, suppression and scrutiny from the in-charge ruling class can be measured by degrees. American MCs deal with helmet laws, aftermarket limits, noise control, motorcycle-only checkpoints, profiling, infiltrators, parole checks, manipulative media, and much more. But in spite of all these authoritative annoyances, at the end of the sea-to-shining-sea day, the clubs remain surrounded by the relative benevolence of red, white, and blue borders. "Issues" may lean hard on US MCs, but looking at all those presidential portraits in the White House, politics aside, none of them really projects the you're-under-my-control hypnotic-eye that we've seen in so many of China's ominous—and once omnipresent—billboard images of Chairman Mao. The latest incarnation of his "official portrait" still gazes thoughtfully over spots such as government buildings and offices, the Tiananmen Gate, and the Forbidden City.

The guy certainly had the look.

When it comes to intimidation, an entire posse of our presidents couldn't brush the lint off the Chairman's Zhongshan–style suit. If fantasy sports extended to world leaders down through history, a face-off between Mao and say, Millard Fillmore, would smack of lunchtime for a Siberian tiger with a paw full of bamboo rat.

And Mao's "look" *doesn't* seem to express a warm, open welcome of one-percenter motorcycle outlaws into his country.

SHOPPING IN THE COMFORT OF YOUR OWN COUNTRY

For openers, getting a Harley in the home of Mao and his successors isn't anywhere near as easy and neat as a visit to one of America's nearly nine hundred boutique-modern factory H-D dealers. Or one of the countless independent shops with used scoots and "former rentals." Or a convenient online shopping experience with comparison pricing and "find-the-motorcycle-of-your-dreams" advanced search.

No.

The evolution of just being able to *ride* a motorcycle in the PRC that is legal-trouble-free is unlike anything Americans and many others in various spots on the globe can begin to understand.

Even Peter Fonda's classic plea for justice in *The Wild Angels*: "We wanna be free! We wanna be free to do what we wanna do. We wanna be free to ride. We wanna be free to ride our machines without being hassled by The Man!" seems watery-and-weak when compared to "The Man" that Clay Jones has to contend with. Think about *his* chronicles of biker life in the PRC the next time you have to suffer through a couple hours' worth of paperwork torture at your local Department of Motor Vehicles, or have to face the growls of your community sheriff with a ticket book in his hand.

"SHARE THE ROAD" WITH COPS AND CORN

The beginning of Clay's two-wheeled adventures in the PRC involved a complex legal and cultural fusion:

> When I arrived in China, tags were nearly impossible to get, so most bikes were ridden "outlaw" with no legal status. Foreigners often smuggled bikes in through Hong Kong or bought existing bikes from expats who were leaving.
>
> I had a Shovel that I traded, along with a little cash, for a twin-cam from a "black" Harley dealer. "Black" in front of any business denotes that the owner has no business license.
>
> I started to ride with the one guy I found—also a foreigner—who was one of the only guys whom I could tell had lived "da life"

back across the big pond. We both had our own tales to not tell as to the circumstances that led us to take up residence here.

On one of our early rides—before the establishment of the MC—we were headed to a section of the Wall. We were cruising along at a good clip when I noticed a crowd of "dirty thunder" approaching our tailpipes fast. The roads in China are not very clean; the locals often use them for drying corn for livestock, which puts a lot of dust particles in the air, making visibility poor.

As we continued on, a car whipped in front of us and the group closed in. Feeling a bit apprehensive, I slowed to see if the group would flash by, but to my disappointment, with the exception of one rider, they fell in behind me and my road dog.

That one rider—whose name I later learned was Qu—motioned for us to pull over. As I negotiated the loose gravel at the road's edge, I saw a girl out of the side of my eye, holding a camera with a massive lens. I also noticed several other people in the car directly in front of me and my partner.

Qu asked where we were going, which I told him in the best Chinese I could muster. With a flip of the hand, he indicated for us to proceed. I offered him the lead position, which he declined, obviously preferring to watch our riding style—which he would later compare to that of an American cowboy, although my partner was Canadian!

We reached our destination and I learned that this group was a club of sorts and that a good portion of them were law officers. I was nervous due to the quasi-legal status of my bike and tag and was somewhat baffled as to why they weren't checking numbers and paperwork. That's when I found out that they, too, were on bikes that weren't legal.

Even the cops ride "outlaw" in the PRC.

A VIRGIN CANVAS FOR MCS AND THE LIFESTYLE

Shortly after his encounter with the cloud of dirty thunder, Clay began the Long March Motorcycle Club (LMMC) as a powerhouse promotion of brotherhood within unique borders. It included both Americans and Chinese and, of course, all of the proper protocol, respect, and caution that is universally required was followed.

But one of the most fascinating twists in Clay's formation of the club was the jettisoning of this lifestyle into a time machine. The PRC is a virgin canvas for motorcycle clubs and patches, and for those with a hard commitment to the lifestyle. It's so globally ironic that while many nations' governments are tightening the garrotes on the throats of bikers, in China, all that club-focused negativity simply doesn't exist. The purity of the brotherhood—and the good old intrinsic fun—is what's being examined and experienced.

Explains Clay:

> Since big-engine bikes are something of a new addition to the culture, and correspondingly, so are clubs, less attention has been paid by authorities to the newly formed MCs and RCs. Some clubs have even been formed by "motocycle" shops as a way to market their bikes, shiny doodads, and aftermarket parts.
>
> And even though Beijing is central to the power base, providential government is often left with the task of enforcement as well as implementation of motorcycle regulations based on local laws. National laws, such as the ones we're seeing in other countries, may not be possible to implement or enforce due to the lack of administration to deal with groups that are not a direct threat to the government.
>
> Another factor is size—size matters in China and large groups require registration and licensing, while smaller groups usually fly under the radar.
>
> And the advent of independent riding groups is so new that no real distinction has been made between two- or three-piece patches and one-percenters. One of the goals of the Long March MC is to encourage the distinction in patches as to levels of dedication to a motorcycle club lifestyle—those in a three-piece patch club being viewed as more dedicated to the procedure and protocol of the lifestyle.
>
> One of the reasons the LMMC keeps a high profile is to quell any questions as to our intentions: that we are a club formed to promote brotherhood and two-wheel fun. In interviews and other forums, I illustrate my close friendship with my Chinese brothers and a freedom based on riding a "motocycle," which in turn illustrates freedom of thought without political threats to the status quo of "The Party."

Another of the strong draws toward the LMMC has a direct correlation to the political climate in the PRC; a draw that is something special "over there," but just a part of life in the United States.

Clay continues:

> The idea of one man, one vote is also attractive to a cultural
> system that has always been "boss" driven; therefore, the average
> person does not find it hard to support a club such as ours that is
> independent of dealerships, exclusive in membership, and requires
> dedication—even if the majority of the riders in China have far
> too many family and employment obligations to consider seeking
> membership in LMMC. Also, by assisting in the formation of RCs,
> we have avoided any complaints or accusations and instead have
> gained support as a credible organization that promotes club culture
> and brotherhood.
>
> At present, the focus of biker-related laws and enforcement
> is on unlicensed bikes and non-licensed riders. MCs are generally
> viewed as a non-threat. Keeping a lower profile of activities while
> keeping a high visibility of stated purpose has also kept MCs out of
> government scrutiny.
>
> But I also realize that at some point all honeymoons end.

"Sweet Home Beijing": Alabama-born Clay Jones, founder of the PRC's Long March MC. *Courtesy of H. Clay Jones, Long March MC*

CRUSHED OR EXPORTED? A CHOKING CHOICE

While the "non-threat" of MCs continues in its careful calm, the technical crackdown on "visitors" and vehicles never gets any easier. As time has rolled on, Clay Jones has received an extensive education in Asian socio-political wrangling, especially in terms of his club; the status of Americans in China (and foreigners in general); ever-tightening registration laws; and dizzying where-you-can-ride-and-when restrictions and regulations.

He has also learned how strongly the lifestyle appeals to native Chinese riders—riders who have become the primary population of the LMMC.

"The LMMC has become more diverse in recent years, with the addition of a loosely constructed support club," says Clay, adding more details to the club's cultural connection. "'74 Support,' named in homage to the LMMC's 'Gear and Dragon' centerpatch. This support club has no official capacity and is not a pathway to membership, but rather an informational group designed to facilitate direct communication between Chinese club members and Chinese riders who are attracted to a biker lifestyle.

"The decision to focus on expanding a support base among Chinese riders was developed in response to the increasingly draconian admin policies of the Chinese government as to foreigner involvement. It's all more difficult due to stricter regulations dealing with visa applications and further complicated by costly number-plate procurement."

And here's where things get *really* complicated!

Clay goes on to unravel the circuitous circus of Beijing's many roads and rules:

> To explain this further, Beijing stopped issuing Jing A number plates, which are required to enter the 4th ring road—a controlled-access expressway in Beijing, which runs around the city. Therefore, a free market has developed for the sale of these number plates.
>
> It's necessary to buy a bike with a number plate, often a small-engined cheap Chinese brand, so you can then crush that bike and receive a permission certificate to tag a new motorcycle. Another method is to buy a legally registered motorcycle that has some of its eleven-year shelf-life left—before requirements dictate that it be crushed or exported!
>
> There are a lot of reasons for these mandates, ranging from environmental to image. When the restrictions were put into place in the mid-'80s, only registration of 150cc or smaller bikes was allowed. No big bikes were really around except for the Chang Jiang sidecar with a 750cc 23hp engine, and those were for official army

and police use only. And the small bikes were seen as transport for farmers and low-income earners, or were utilized as getaway vehicles for purse snatchers! That led to complete motorcycle bans in some cities.

Then you have the economics: as auto production increased so did profit margins on their sales, increasing government tax revenues. Environmentally, it made a kind of sense to crush the Chinese-made bikes, as the engine tech was old and not eco-friendly.

Finally, "face" is very important in China. And as an international first-tier city, Beijing wanted to push an image of improvement; motorcycles sporting farmers and the working class did not project the same image as sophisticates in slick BMW sedans!

But now is now and we can have the big bikes. But as we've seen, they're expensive and licensing them is bureaucratically exhausting.

The current cost for a Jing A number plate is around US$16,500!

In the past, we could get a foreign company to buy a Jing B number plate, which would at least allow operation outside the 4th ring road of Beijing. However, foreign companies are no longer allowed to purchase these plates, so they must be bought by a Chinese citizen who resides outside of Beijing proper.

The cost of a Jing B is lower, at around US$900.

Motorcycles legally registered outside of Beijing are not allowed inside the 6th ring road. This in effect takes the cultural pursuit of a motorcycle lifestyle out of the possibilities of the normal worker who makes a standard Chinese working wage—unless the individual is totally dedicated to owning and riding a motorcycle.

The cultural phenomenon that was born with the black-market importation of Harley-Davidsons has thus been replaced by riders who have deep pockets and are members of the nouveau riche. These so-called "Rolex riders" are typically not good club members, as the motorcycle then becomes a symbol of opulence instead of freedom.

Adding to the money end of all this is that somewhere around 2010, Harley began legal importation of motorcycles. Harley has since pressured law enforcement to impound those bikes not legally registered. For sales, Harley dealers naturally target these deep-pocket "bikers," as they drive up profits with their predilections for those shiny doodads; they can often be seen hunkered down around the big-screen TV at the local dealer discussing what this or that "authorized" add-on would cost and what future purchases they would like to make.

RIDER REQUIRED: "A BANKCARD TO FACILITATE THE PAYMENT OF FINES"

Something else to think about: When was the last time you worried about being kicked out of *your* country after receiving a speeding or "fix-it" ticket? Especially during a military-might parade?

During the last two years, Beijing riders have witnessed a crackdown on motorcycles, which includes checkpoints and roadblocks designed to identify those riders who do not have legal bikes or proper driver's licenses. These roadblocks have extended past Beijing city limits into the mountains that surround the city.

In September of 2015, during the celebration marking the "70th anniversary of China's victory in the War of Resistance against Japan" and the 70th anniversary of the end of World War II, which featured a parade to showcase China's military might, the stops were intensified. "Papers" and motorcycle registration were demanded by units stationed along secondary roads with the single mission of detaining riders and impounding motorcycles that did not meet current regulations.

Due to these and other factors, says Clay, LMMC has "gone legal" and club rules state that all members are now required to have legally operational motorcycles.

"Of course, in all reality," Clay admits, "I think we would consider someone who was not one hundred percent legal, but we have taken the public stand of 'legal is better.'"

Further crackdown on motorcycle-related activity has come in the form of additional tactics to trap motorcycles in the city with surprise stoplight detainment to inspect the motorcycle for legal paperwork to include insurance and registration—which also dictates the rider to possess a bankcard to facilitate the payment of fines. Additional regulations include an increase in points and fines leveled by camera enforcement and the possibility of a loss of license, which in a foreigner's case could result in deportation.

"THERE CAN BE NO DEMOCRACY WITHOUT V-TWINS!"

How has this affected the Long March Motorcycle Club?

Clay reveals that the club's foreign members have had to leave China due to visa difficulties and employment requirements, thereby shifting the membership to mostly Chinese nationals. Adding in the club's lengthy prospecting process—as long as two years—the LMMC has developed into a tightly knit unit of brotherhood.

"It took a club effort to achieve legal status for all members' motorcycles," Clay expands, "and, along with 74 Support members, we have begun to join Asian-related events such as the BMW GS Trophy Challenge 2016, and recently LMMC members took third place in the regional."

The LMMC has developed ties with local landmark businesses that cater to the motorcycle culture, such as Ace Cafe, and the club was invited to participate at their opening as well as the Ducati Scrambler unveiling in China.

Overall, the LMMC appears to be here to stay and to serve as a motivational organization to develop club culture and universal biker brotherhood in a land of continual cultural revolution and evolution. The club, Clay hopes, will also promote motorcycle awareness and the general idea of assistance and integrity.

Says Clay: "There can be no democracy without V-twins!"

FREEDOM OF THOUGHT, LESSONS IN BROTHERHOOD

So maybe those V-twins are helping. Maybe this new revolution is aiding in the mellowing of the old one. Since putting on the big targets of a three-piece patch, Clay has eased smartly but surely onto the rough and sometimes low-visibility road of Chinese acceptance—by government and by the people.

And it has worked.

Along with a slow, moderate, and watchful acceptance of Western social creep, the controlling hypnotic eye even winks now and then. Clay and his brothers have been featured in several Chinese motorcycle publications and globally published books.

The Long March MC has established clout and cred.

In August 2015, ChinaDaily.com broadcast a video interview with Clay that— complete with a biker-twang rock 'n' roll soundtrack—could have easily been a laidback, sunny segment in a Sturgis, Daytona, or Anywhere, USA–based fun-doc. Far removed from the tormenting tenseness of 1989's Tiananmen Square footage, Clay certainly wasn't under the gun of a Type 59 tank as he freely discussed with interviewer Huan Cao the theories and methods of *his* revolution and just what this one-percenter lifestyle is all about to him:

> I've been in Bejing ten or eleven years, but I've been in China for
> fifteen. Bigger motorcycles gave way to a lifestyle; a motorcycle
> lifestyle. A biker lifestyle is one of freedom and freedom of thought.
> [When] you get on a motorcycle and head in a direction, anything
> is possible.
>
> One of the goals that I had when I came to China was to be
> able to ride a motorcycle. I founded the motorcycle club as an idea
> of creating safety in motorcycling, education in motorcycling, and
> also brotherhood.

And brotherhood is different than friendship. Within a motorcycle club you might have your friends, but everyone within the club is a brother. That means at three o'clock in the morning [if] that person needs help, then you get up out of bed and you go take care of it and you take care of the business that needs to be taken care of that time. If they have a flat tire, you go get them; if they run out of gas, you take them a can of gas; if they need money, you bring them money.

The guys I ride with are the best guys in the world. There's no better. They're my friends and they're Chinese.

NOW, ABOUT THAT SAFETY AND EDUCATION STUFF...

Then things got a little less philosophic and a little more practical.

In China, Clay told Huan Cao,

[T]he respect level for motorcycles is lower. [That's] dangerous, because...for example, [people] don't really understand that a motorcycle needs a lot of time to stop. Somebody will step out in front of you and throw their hand up, not realizing that they may be causing a dangerous situation for themselves and the rider as well. Patience and respect are what will help to create safe roadways and safe riding and driving in China.

"Patience and respect"—hmm, two good rules to follow. Whether you're zig-zagging around pedestrians in Chinese streets, sliding around remote roads of loose gravel and dry corn, or living out the universal principle of brotherhood in a land that's still learning.

MO' BIKER REFERENCES FROM MAO

Clay closed his China Daily interview with a couple of questions.

And a very open-ended answer: "People always ask me why I didn't *leave* China more than they ask why I *came* to China. 'Why haven't you left China?' they want to know. Primarily, all my friends are Chinese and I've lived here a long time. I have several motorcycles, I have a nice place to live, and I have a life in China. That's the reason I stay here."

Talking with the "P" of the Long March MC calls to mind one more apropos axiom from Mao: "*People like me sound like a lot of big cannons.*"

Clay Jones certainly does.

Special and pioneering people like him have a big sound all their own. What Clay has accomplished thunders like Mao's cannons and roars louder than straight pipes on a 110-incher.

He adds so much to the boom of biker brotherhood, now truly heard 'round—and in a very unlikely corner of—the world.

REACTION AND RESPONSE

Yep! Since 2009, American Clay Jones's Long March MC has pioneered, prospered, and proliferated in the PRC. It's a whole new kind of "Cultural Revolution," to which more of Mao's words of wisdom may apply: "In waking a tiger, use a long stick."

CHAPTER 11:

EINE ROCKERLEGENDE AUS BERLIN

THE ENIGMA OF LOMMEL AND GERMANY'S BORN TO BE WILD MC

INTERROGATING THE SUBJECT

Isn't every major motorcycle club beyond US borders a part
of or associated with one of the top-tier established American MCs?

Whenever I put my club vest on I don't look like a lawyer or a bank clerk, and I cannot nor do I want to hide like everyone. That is my life!

—Lommel, *A Rocker Legend from Berlin*

There is one myth, mystery, and rumor of the one-percent culture that can be quickly crushed. It's the assumption—especially by newer riders—that all the world's monster-sized MCs emanated from the US.

It just ain't so.

Sure, all of this started on stateside roads, and there's no denying that America was responsible for the initial worldwide growth of the lifestyle. The list of clubs that have expanded out from fast and fertile American soil has become long; most of the big boys, and plenty of others at various positions on the leaderboard, have become *sehr international*. Borders became transparent as the one-percenter lifestyle ghost-walked its spirit into country after country after country, settling in and getting comfortable.

But then diversity hit. Mighty clubs formed and flourished overseas, independent of US ties. Other clubs began to bypass a US presence altogether as they developed in places such as Asia, spreading throughout Thailand, Singapore, Japan, and Hong Kong. Or Australia, where one MC took the big-pond border-leap directly into Norway.

But it is in major world cities that indigenous motorcycle clubs have set themselves up as massive regional powers.

"MORAL PANIC" FROM THE INSIDE

One of the biggest homegrown MCs—established and led by a man named Lommel—is Germany's Born to be Wild, founded in Berlin in the 1970s. "The Borns" have a long, legendary history; a large support club network; and a founder with *über* charisma.

Among other talents, Lommel is an author, with a couple of books to his credit. But apart from all the colorful and crazed entertainment he provides, Lommel has presented two especially hard-hitting history lessons. One, he has provided a parallel chronicle of what the biker/one-percenter scene was like in Germany as it skidded and sped out of the 1960s. America may have been dealing with Vietnam, drugs, pain-in-the-ass politics, hippies versus bikers, and so much more social bedlam, but Europe was also experiencing chaos-of-change.

Lommel's alliance with the "rocker" side of the Euro youth image really shows a living out of what sociologists back then called "moral panic."

And what Lommel has presented through his annals is a look at this lifestyle through that elusive and exclusive from-the-inside position—something that is forever a truth-struggle in the US as well as everywhere else.

Dating back to the 1970s, Germany's Born to be Wild MC is a major force in the Euro-biker universe. *Courtesy of Lommel, Born to be Wild MC*

The guy has had his boots on the ground through it all, and he has no problem laying out the details—from the early bailing-wire-and-hope bikes, to being in and out of other clubs, to arrests and imprisonment, to all that it has taken to keep a 1% MC growing and strong for decades.

And he's proud of his writing method, too.

I want to tell those guys who know the scene from the 70s to the 21st century very well, that I wrote it down the way I experienced and remembered everything. Actually I did not keep a diary or anything similar. That is pussy like.

—Lommel

DAS ORIGINAL MOTORCYCLE JAMBOREE

In the early 1990s, Lommel and his BTBWMC put together an event that has also had quite a *lange Lebensdauer*. Their Motorcycle Jamboree is a giant, with an annual attendance of around twenty thousand.

The summer fun began in the town of Biesenthal, thirty-one kilometers northeast of Berlin; then the run marched into historic Jüterbog on the Nuthe River. Jüterbog has endured the Saxons, the Napoleonic Wars, the Nazis, and even the Red Army, so dealing with twenty thousand bikers is a piece of *Kuchen*.

The Jamboree, like so much of BTBW's support merchandise, is marketed under the club's brand, Wild Power; and a full-on brand it is. Lommel and BTBW have muscled up through their own German history and through their own native-land social struggles to form a brotherhood that is distinctly their own through and through.

In 2005, a German biker magazine published a feature about the club's thirtieth anniversary, ending the article with the perfect sign of German love and respect: "*Doch jetzt ist es Zeit mit den Borns anzustoßen und ihnen für die nächsten Jahre alles Gute zu wünschen!*"

"But now it's time to drink a toast to the Borns and to wish them all the best for the future!"

Pass the Kölsch...*Prost!*

REACTION AND RESPONSE

Certainly plenty of small indigenous clubs exist beyond America's borders, but major and powerful clubs of non-US origin also exist, advance, and make a worldwide impact. Germany's Born to be Wild MC is a *perfektes Beispiel.*

CHAPTER 12:

THE "RUNNING-OUT-OF-CONTROL TRIBE"

THE STRANGE RISE AND FALL OF JAPAN'S *BŌSŌZOKU*

INTERROGATING THE SUBJECT

Are the *bōsōzoku* actually kind of an anime cartoon or
are they a legitimate part of biker culture history?

Japan's motorcycle gangs or bosozoku... aren't anything like American motorcycle gangs. Or at least, not anymore.... major elements of today's bosozoku still harken back to the glory days of post-WWII American teenage rebellion: pompadour hairstyles, greaser attire, impromptu weapons, and really obnoxious attitudes. Bosozoku members are typically between the ages of 16 and 20... They have never really been adult-oriented groups like many American motorcycle gangs.

—Kat Callahan, *Jalopnik*, October 10, 2014

About six thousand miles west of America's sprawling soil, the sun rises on a very different land. With its own *tokubetsu* take on industrial intensity and social passion, Japan has been intimate with the motorcycle culture for years.

Nippon-koku ("the State of Japan") has spent a generation or two involved in high-tech intercourse, breeding lookalike Harley clones: big twins like Honda VTXs and Shadows; Kawasaki Vulcans; and Yamaha's entire assortment of Stars, Strykers, Stratoliners, Raiders, Roadstars, and V Stars.

Their *cultural* coitus has also been lubed with American and other outside influences, but as the Japanese absorbed bikes into their blood, a few over-the-top leaps into looniness would dwarf even the observation platform at the Tokyo Skytree.

WAITING IN THE KAMIKAZE LINE

At the heaving heart of Japan's motorcycle madness were the *bōsōzoku*—literally translated as "running-out-of-control tribes" or "violent speed tribes." The term also stands as the rough Japanese-language equivalent of OMG.

When I was in Japan, I actually met a member of the "Lighting Tribe" in Shimizu-ku. [F]riggin bikes they rode were trippin. NOT really a 1% club per say [*sic*], mostly street racer punks. Wild stuff....
—Comment about bōsōzoku on motobrick.com, February 2012

Bōsōzoku began in the 1950s, and here is where an especially sideways counterpart connection with American biker heritage exists. US World War II vets came home to a life of difficult mainstream assimilation that put them in the saddles of big bikes. Well, Japanese vets did the same. Except a lot of *them* were kamikaze pilots who just didn't quite have the honored opportunity to fly that one last mission.

That's a rough pressure cooker of a queue to be jumping in and out of.

Bosozoku's roots date back to the post WWII years when a new societal problem group arose. Having lived under the war-time rule and even an assumption of never returning home alive, such as the kamikaze pilots assigned for a mission that never came to be, some of the war veterans could not return to peaceful life without difficulties. The most extreme of these individuals started looking for new excitement by tuning cars and conducting less-than-desired gang-type activities on city streets. Inspiration and idols were found from foreign movies such as *Rebel Without a Cause* (1955). These ideologies later caught the motorcycle-obsessed youth, and bosozoku was born.

—4into1.com

FASHION-FORWARD IN PUNCH PERMS

In 1976, director Mitsuo Yanagimachi created one of the more interesting biker-based documentaries ever filmed. On sixteen-millimeter black-and-white film, his ninety-minute *God Speed You! Black Emperor* follows a bōsōzoku club, the Black Emperors, doing what they did best in those days: riding in huge loud groups, running tollbooths, blowing traffic signals, ignoring cops, smashing cars and threatening the passengers, and just in general living up to the translation of bōsōzoku—violent, running out-of-control.

Shortly after that, bōsōzoku entered the '80s and what has been called its "golden age." The excesses of Kabuki theatre have nothing on what bōsōzoku brought to the stage of Japan's swarming streets. American cops may have patches to analyze, exhaust thunder to decibelize, and the occasional handlebar shotgun to neutralize, but the bōsōzoku really turned it on for Nippon's finest.

The bōsōzoku waved imperial Japanese flags, wooden swords, metal pipes, and baseball bats; they threw Molotov cocktails and other deadly debris. The bikes—a wacky wonderland of shapes and sizes—had screaming paint and kamikaze kitsch, along with cartoon-exaggerated fins, fairings, "Christmas lights," and pipes.

The riders themselves were right out of an anime dream—or nightmare: jumpsuits, *tokkō-fuku* ("kamikaze attack uniforms"), outfits often described colorfully (online and elsewhere) as "overcoats with kanji slogans usually worn open with no shirt underneath showing off their bandaged torsos and baggy matching pants tucked inside tall boots," sashes tied in an *X* around their guts, full leather suits, round sunglasses, long headbands called *hachimaki*, pompadours, and some kind of hairdo called the "punch perm." The signature surgical mask rounded out the ensemble. You could almost hear Tim Gunn on *Project Runway* setting up bōsōzoku night: "Gather 'round, designers! You'll have eight hours to complete this 'violent speed'–look challenge, using only these materials taken from a dumpster behind the Pokémon Museum."

DECAYING LIKE A FORGOTTEN HODAKA IN A BARN

In 1982, Japanese authorities estimated that over forty-two thousand bikers were involved in motorcycle "gangs"—including bōsōzoku in that count. In 2011, the Japanese National Police dropped the estimate to below ten thousand, "the lowest number since the collection of data on the gangs began in 1975." In 2012 it was reported by authorities that the number of "gangs" in the Tokyo area was now 119, down from 5,300 in 1980.

So what happened to the bōsōzoku? How in the world could biker-epochal things such as Suzuki GSX 400s with aftermarket rocket-ship trim, jumpsuits, surgical riding masks, and boulevard-clogging mass-mayhem with a kamikaze heritage simply fade away like a long-forgotten Hodaka 90 in a Hokkaido barn?

Well, there seem to be a couple of good reasons: money and cops. Always two important factors in limiting freedom and fun.

> Two major [factors] seem to explain the decline in bosozoku participation. Ironically, one of the biggest might be the worsening of the Japanese economy. While this would at first seem counterintuitive, as one would expect the economic effects of the prolonged recession and deflation such as falling wages, casualisation of work, higher unemployment, and increased taxes would lead to a burgeoning of a protest social class like the bosozoku. Instead, those now being actively recruited into the bosozoku crews most likely have substantially less money than their peers of the bubble economy. Bikes are expensive, and modifications even more so....New recruits are now often wearing street clothes and riding cheap scooters....
>
> The second reason for the decline is likely the increased measures taken by the National Police Agency....new police vehicles currently have cameras in them, and so when you see the police following bikers without apparently doing much of anything, what's really happening is they're collecting enough evidence for identification purposes later. The general public doesn't see the arrests, because they happen after the police analyse the video and identify perpetrators. While it still didn't sound like arrested members of the bosozoku go to prison (which is a very, very good thing, because Japanese prisons are horrible and no place to put teenagers or really anyone for that matter convicted of small scale crimes), [a police] spokesman did make it clear that convictions are extremely costly and negatively affect the driving record.
>
> —Kat Callahan, jalopnik.com, October 10, 2014

So bōsōzoku tribes are trickling out.

The flamboyance is fading fast.

But maybe that's how it should be in the overall this-lifestyle-is-not-for-everyone scheme of things—big numbers often reflect a fad; smaller numbers reflect the committed.

And the committed in Japan now include serious chapters of major established MCs—ones that are heavy on the outlaw diamond patches and light on the punch perms.

HAVING A COLD ONE IN THE "BARIBARIAN SPACECRAFT"

One far-out last gasp of bōsōzoku outrageousness came with the help of the always-fad-fixated entertainment industry. They squeezed out some vicarious wasabi with the late '90s TV series *Gekisou Sentai Carranger*, the show adapted into the American *Power Rangers* in which the main group of villains is the Space Bōsōzoku Bowzock, an intergalactic biker gang that has, according to reports about the show, "no respect of traffic laws" and "hang[s] out at the BB Saloon, a bar in the Baribarian spacecraft."

"Wow, Red Racer!"

Now, while all that anti-society and drinking stuff may be a little negative, it's enlightening to see perhaps a touch of prophecy here, expanding the biker culture to intergalactic status. The show is also quite the shivering climax to a part of this lifestyle that, at its most fertile peak, was in its own weird way pretty damn potent.

REACTION AND RESPONSE

The bōsōzoku seem to be an Asian fusion of cartoon and culture. Now that their numbers are in a kamikaze descent, studies of them lean more toward history than current hipness. But there's no denying that their place in worldwide biker lore is unquestionably unique and head-shakingly bizarre.

Out of control! Violent! Fast! Two film documentaries, *God Speed You! Black Emperor* and *Sayonara Speed Tribes*—produced thirty-six years apart—have chronicled the mythic and mysterious world of Japan's long-lived bōsōzoku.

CHAPTER 13:

"PUTIN'S ANGELS"

THROWING THE SEPARATION OF MC AND STATE TO THE WOLVES

INTERROGATING THE SUBJECT

Does Russia's Night Wolves MC really work with and for their country's government? If so, does this represent an anomaly never before seen in the lifestyle? I mean, aren't the "authorities" and clubs natural enemies?

Grabovo, Ukraine—A Malaysia Airlines Boeing 777 with 298 people aboard exploded, crashed and burned on a flowered wheat field Thursday in a part of eastern Ukraine controlled by pro-Russia separatists, blown out of the sky at 33,000 feet by what Ukrainian and American officials described as a Russian-made antiaircraft missile.

—*The New York Times*, July 17, 2014

T he bloody crash-and-burn head butting between Vladimir Putin's Russia and the torn-in-two Ukraine has crushed more than just skulls and spirit. It perfectly defines "countries in chaos."

It also perfectly defines the violent endgame of power and politics—two apparently inherent human needs that *occasionally* flare up within the ranks of motorcycle clubs as well. So it's really no surprise that an MC would have at least some type of connection to the action. After all, in 1960s America, motorcycle clubs weren't shy about voicing their differences with the hippies and the rest of society regarding the Vietnam War, pacifism, draft dodging, flowers in gun barrels, and all things soft and sweet.

And they have never backed away from their chasm of distrust with the government; *that* enemy was locked in from the beginning. Legislation such as RICO and the Patriot Act has fractured the fissure for good.

But what is a surprise—a curiosity just boiling over with myths, mysteries, and rumors—is the connection between the Russian-born Night Wolves MC and its government. The pair's interaction is unlike anything ever seen within the biker world. We are confronted with the puzzle of a world-class MC being deeply, *deeply* in bed— кровати—with the lawmakers and law enforcers of their country. It's something that defies nature; it's water flowing uphill.

It's borscht on burger buns at a backyard barbeque.

"CLUB BUSINESS" TAKEN TO NEW LEVELS

Formed from the times and trials of the illegal and censored Russian music scene of the 1980s, the Night Wolves Motorcycle Club rose to become the "first official bike club in the USSR."

The brand grew from there.

Racing teams, custom shops (Wolf Engineering), tattoo parlors, rock concerts, night clubs, clothing lines (Wolf Wear), and plans to manufacture their own motorcycle (Wolf-Ural) have made the MC ultra-high-profile and unique. Throw in the fact that they are now riding buddies with Vladimir Putin, engage in actual combat missions for the state, and receive funding from the Kremlin, the organization appears to lean more toward being a *bureau* than a bike club.

But maybe that's because the concept of "nationalism" is a whole lot different in Russia than it is in other parts of the planet—especially the US.

Maybe.

THE DOCTOR IS IN

In October 2015, *Rolling Stone* published Damon Tabor's inquisitive, in-depth piece about the club, much of it focusing on Alexander Zaldostanov, known as "The Surgeon." Zaldostanov, a former dental surgeon, became the Night Wolves's leader of the pack in 1989 and remains well-entrenched in that position. His color of nationalism goes far beyond good old red-blooded patriotism: a love of country above and apart from whatever governmental entity may be in power. The Surgeon and the Night Wolves are committed to the complete Russian package—lock, stock, and ideology—from Putin on down.

> After his swim, the Surgeon strides over to a replica World War II fighter plane. A battle tank, imported from a film studio in Kazakhstan, sits parked nearby in the scrub grass. Both would be incorporated into the Night Wolves bike show in several weeks — a phantasmagorical spectacle celebrating the Red Army's victory over Hitler and intended to feed Russia's growing Soviet nostalgia. "I'm very excited by the topic of war at the moment," the Surgeon says. "I'm not fucking interested in show just for show. I'm a warrior. I'm fighting for my country, for my history. I'm talking about what Russia is facing now. Especially America, putting the shit on it."
>
> —Damon Tabor,
> "Putin's Angels: Inside Russia's Most Infamous Motorcycle Club,"
> October 8, 2015, *Rolling Stone*

The Surgeon is obviously outspoken. He's as widely quoted as any politician, and he and his club's views are well-known. There is no mystery when it comes to their praise of Stalin ("For the Motherland! For Stalin!"), their anti-homosexual stance ("death to faggots"), their anti-West views ("global Satanism"), and their involvement with the Russian Orthodox Church (with "runs" that are pilgrimages to holy Russian Orthodox sites).

Even though the club—now freely said to be five thousand members strong—is explicitly patterned after major Western MCs, *Rolling Stone* also reported that the Surgeon "has now become an outspoken detractor of so-called outlaw clubs. In the Russian press, he has called them 'arms dealers,' 'demons' and 'drug cartels on wheels.' In June, the Surgeon asked Russia's parliament to include [two of the Big Five American MCs] on the government's new list targeting 'undesirable' foreign organizations."

And entertainment can be "undesirable," too. It's a safe bet that no Wolves have Russia's Pussy Riot "feminist punk rock protest group" on their iPods.

> "I want us to remain a patriotic club, to be an example for the young, to do something for our Fatherland–which we basically lost by buying jeans and chewing gum, selling out for McDonald's," Zaldostanov said. "The Night Wolves are a phenomenon—bigger than a motorbike club, something that makes presidents come to us and the Patriarch give us his blessing."
>
> The Night Wolves supported the Orthodox church last year during the Pussy Riot controversy. After the feminist group performed their "punk prayer" in Moscow's Christ the Savior Cathedral in February 2012, the club publicly expressed outrage and then promised to help guard Orthodox cathedrals from any further "hooliganism."
>
> —Yaroslava Kiryukhina, December 8, 2013,
> *Russia Beyond the Headlines*

COUNTER-COUNTERCULTURE?

The mystery in all this comes in that nagging defying of nature. How can two factions that are inherent enemies in every other setting settle into a cozy comradeship just across the Red border? The snake and the mongoose are going to tear each other to shreds whether they're in South Africa or South Carolina. In *most* forever-feuds, safe havens and "no bullying zones" simply don't exist.

But is the Putin-Wolf coupling really a sincere and rare breed of nationalism, or is it something much more complex—and political?

In May 2015, *the Moscow Times* published an op-ed by Mark Galeotti, professor of global affairs at New York University. The article, with the slightly leading title of "An Unusual Friendship: Bikers and the Kremlin," was accompanied by a satirically brutal political cartoon of Putin in a dog-walking posture; but mutts weren't at the end of his leashes, tiny motorcycles were. A half dozen of them. All ridden by little wolves with flaming heads.

That gave the reader a pretty good idea where this was going; and Galeotti's point was made quickly:

> Putin has several times ridden with the Wolves (albeit on a trike) and in 2013 awarded their leader, Alexander Zaldostanov, the Order of Honor.

Considering that this is a group which was founded in the 1980s as a counterculture movement, that claims to reject the law, and which has been involved in gang clashes with other motorcycle groups, this may seem paradoxical.

However, in practice the Wolves are nowhere near as rebellious as they may appear, for all their chromed hogs and studded leathers. Instead, they are in many ways a case study in the Kremlin's strategy of adopting and taming potentially hostile groups and using them precisely as tools of control—counter-counterculture, as it were.

And Galeotti never lets up; he pounds home the case that the Night Wolves are "auxiliaries of the state," useful as "a potential militia at home," and "a leading light in the 'Anti-Maidan' movement to oppose liberal protests in the street."

There is, of course, no First Amendment in Russia.

Then Galeotti wraps things up by referring to the club as "outlaws yet tools of the state."

Op-eds are never supposed to be subtle, but this one swings an especially heavy hammer and sickle. And who's correct here? Galeotti and his educated skepticism, or is the Surgeon really that powerful of a leader with a passionate nationalism that "makes presidents come to us"?

Most haunting for both sides, though, is Galeotti's comments about the "Kremlin's strategy of adopting and taming potentially hostile groups and using them precisely as tools of control." For generations, the US government—on federal, state, and local levels—has been trying to plow clubs under and eliminate them completely. Many other countries—most notably, Australia—have been doing the same. But the Orwell-esque idea of "taming" and "using" clubs for governmental power-purposes might just be the most sinister of all.

And maybe it has already been done.

REACTION AND RESPONSE

Da! Yes! Motorcycle clubs working not only closely, but even as agents of a country's government, is unheard of. And, according to some experts, it's especially dangerous when it involves the possibility that they could be "used." Big Brother and brotherhood are very different things.

PART IV

The Cops

CHAPTER 14:

TAKING THE SHIRT RIGHT OFF YOUR BACK

THE FEDS' PUZZLING PILFERING OF MC PATCHES

INTERROGATING THE SUBJECT

Can law enforcement actually seize everything with a club's name, logo, or reference on it? And do they have the right to literally peel a patch off of someone?

It's comforting to know that local police sniping from gunships is the exception rather than a grisly rule. In fact, *for the most part*, the arsenal used by authorities has drifted heavily from weapons to warrants—less hot lead flying, more legislation and legalities looming. And so much of that is now being done in the relentless pursuit of those pesky one-percenters. Tort tricks that include trademark infringements and localized anti-gang/anti-fraternization ordinances have become the new high-caliber heat.

And after nearly fifty years on the books, 1970's RICO statute is still a go-to favorite. That broad and burning law is exhumed on a regular basis and marched into courtrooms like a hungry, decaying zombie, ever-ready to wreak heavy havoc. RICO's main prosecutorial lever comes in its ability to provide penalties for what is essentially mere association. It's bad and worldwide, having an obvious influence on similar laws in Australia, Canada, Denmark, and other jurisdictions around the globe.

That's a bit tough on club members—clubs are *defined* by association.

"LET'S GET READY TO *RUUMMMMBLE!*"

RICO and other governmental twists of US law made 2008 and 2009 main-event years for the entirety of the MC community.

United States Attorney Thomas P. O'Brien; Federal District Judge Florence-Marie Cooper; the Mongols Motorcycle Club; their former president, Ruben "Doc" Cavazos; Mongol member Ramon Rivera; and others were thrown into the ring for a legislative "loser leave town, battle-royal death match" with a result that could and would affect every patch-wearing club member on the planet.

It was an ugly, long, and creatively complex example of litigious lunacy.

O'Brien had seized or outlawed everything with the Mongols patch, logo, name, or reference on it, maintaining that the club's colors were subject to that seizure, and later forfeiture, under RICO.

An amendment to O'Brien's original restraining order against the wearing of anything associated with the club, dated October 22, 2008, actually contains the following foul language:

> If the subject refuses to voluntarily surrender the item [colors, logo
> apparel, etc.], the officer shall be permitted to seize the item.

All of this action was the culmination of the ATF's three-year investigation of the Mongols MC, officially called Operation Black Rain.

Cavazos was arrested for racketeering as a result of the operation, inciting him to claim ownership of the club's trademarks and reportedly attempt to use them in a plea deal.

On May 15, 2009, Rivera filed Case No. 2:09-cv-2435-FMC-VBKx in United States District Court Central District of California in an attempt to stop the seizures.

The proceedings were passionate, the ramifications resounding.

Eventually, a Judge Cooper figuratively spat in the eye of O'Brien and the ATF by returning the Mongols' patches to their rightful owners. Among the weighty legalese that she laid down in the bottom line of her ruling were a few passages that were pretty easy to understand:

> The use and display of collective membership marks therefore
> directly implicate the First Amendment's right to freedom of
> association. The Supreme Court has recognized that "implicit in
> the right to engage in activities protected by the First Amendment"
> is "a corresponding right to associate with others in pursuit of a
> wide variety of political, social, economic, educational, religious,
> and cultural ends." This right is crucial in preventing the majority
> from imposing its views on groups that would rather express other,
> perhaps unpopular, ideas. Furthermore, clothing identifying one's
> association with an organization is generally considered expressive
> conduct entitled to First Amendment protection. . . .

Amen.

ALL'S NOT NECESSARILY WELL THAT SORT OF ENDS WELL

Unfortunately, the judge's statements did not bring an end to the persecution—the feds have not given up. And the clash continues to subject even the most sacred sections of the United States Constitution to folds and mutilation.

I've said it before, and I'll say it again, gang members have no civil rights...Mongols, do not come to the city of Lancaster. We will direct law enforcement to incarcerate you....We do not want you. We will not tolerate your presence...[Mongols] are engaged in domestic terrorism...and they kill our children.

—R. Rex Parris, Mayor of Lancaster, California,
as reported in articles in the *Antelope Valley Press*
and other California media outlets, July 2009

Parris may be considered a lot of things, but subtle isn't one of them. The same goes for many of his peers, buddy bureaucrats, and those in law enforcement when it comes to bikers.

If I have a biker in Hollister breaking the law, he is going to jail.... Honestly, they all need to go to prison—all of them.

—Curtis Hill, former Sheriff of San Benito County,
home of Hollister, as reported in the *Hollister Free Lance*,
September 9, 2010

THE PATCH YOU SAVE MAY BE YOUR OWN

A few years after the original federal frying, the authorities were at it again; twisting technicalities and latching onto loopholes. This time the club filed their own complaint.

The Mongols claim the government has re-launched RICO forfeiture proceedings despite the [previous] ruling because the club dissolved and reincorporated in April 2012....Since the government failed in its attempt to seize their marks in [the previous ruling], the Mongols say, it has no right to seize them now just because the club has a new name and its marks are pending trademark approval under that name...."Here, the government attempts to re-litigate the same issue with what it will construe as a different party," the complaint states.

—Courthouse News Service, June 20, 2014

Those attacks by the feds generated multi-MC "Save the Patch" rallies; everyone was aware that the government wouldn't stop with one club.

Not by a longshot.

In October 2014, the feds expanded their hunt to include yet another major American MC. And then another.

But there is some hope amidst the tort tricks and twists.

> An amazingly positive thing happened this week when the government's RICO case and attached trademark seizure were dismissed in Federal District Court by Judge David O. Carter . . . as it turns out, the dismissal has nothing to do with the issue of trademark forfeiture at all. In fact, the idea of a RICO dismissal based on disputes over forfeiture were rejected by Judge Carter as premature. The reason the case was dismissed against the Mongols was entirely related to the prosecution's failure to properly conform to RICO requirements.
>
> —Motorcycle Profiling Project, September 18, 2015

Okay, but you can almost see that familiar and lingering last frame from a sci-fi B movie: The end?

Not a chance.

This monster is far from dead.

REACTION AND RESPONSE

At times, law enforcement can seize club property, depending upon the swing and sway of complex court decisions. So, come to think of it, maybe dodging bullets from a high-speed pursuit 'copter every now and then would be easier than the long and expensive attacks that seem to be occurring in the hallowed halls of justice on a daily basis.

The attacks by the feds have generated many multi-MC "Save the Patch" rallies.

CHAPTER 15:

TOY STORY FOREVER, FOREVER *TOY STORY*

BUZZ GETS BUSTED

INTERROGATING THE SUBJECT

Despite the millions in charitable dollars and donations generated
by bikers, do cops really look at holiday toy runs as publicity
stunts—just MCs putting on a jolly, generous face for the public while
bicycles and Barbies cover up the barbarism and the bad?

Visually, toy runs are a ton more fun than even old Saint Nick and his antlers-up known associates jetting along on that Christmas Eve NORAD map. Full-suited Santas on bikes, slutty Mrs. Clauses straddling the back, elf-dogs in side-hacks, and bikes bungied with "lots of toys and goodies," looking like Buzz Lightyear's closet, say a very special kind of "Ho, ho, ho!" That sort of festive freak-out is far more impressive—to some of us, at least—than even the Grand Sweepstakes–winning giant animated-squirrel "American Folk Tail" float at the Rose Parade.

Many of these runs have become regional rites and must-attend events. From benevolent behemoths such as the Big Texas Toy Run to Ohio's Clark County Highway Hikers holiday happening, the Savannah Toy Run, the Christmas-morning bike giveaway in San Diego, and the Skid Row shopping spree in the blistered bowels of L.A.'s mission district, toy runs generate untold bucks in holiday cheer for kids who could otherwise expect variations on lumps-of-coal in their hole-ridden stockings.

Charity runs in general are what bikers—and many clubs—are known for.

It's what they do.

'TWAS THE NIGHT BEFORE THE FIRST TOY RUN

One of the best looks at just when free-range toy-run giving began came from the now-iconic site AgingRebel.com, an inside portal that truly covers bikerdom's good, badass, and occasionally ugly:

> The fine and revered institution of the motorcycle toy run is now in its 35th year.
>
> It all started in the long ago "Biker's Rights" year of 1973.
>
> And, unless you lived through it, you can't begin to imagine how strange life was then. Try to imagine outlaws demonstrating in the streets, chanting, "Stop the helmet law, man! Stop the helmet law now!" Seventy-three was a time when most bikers looked like

hippies, hippies wanted to look like bikers, and bikers and hippies were both held—by the government, by the FBI, by Nixon, by Middle America—in the same low regard.

Now the hippies are all United States Senators and we are all still scooter trash. And, like us, the toy run will simply not go away.

No, neither will go away. Although *some* would prefer that both disappear.

"YOU'RE A MEAN ONE, OFFICER GRINCH..."

So here we go. Once again, the biker community finds itself in a polarizing pickle. Evidently, it's tough for some segments of society to see people they don't like or don't agree with having fun and helping folks.

First, some samplings from citizens:

> Time for sheriff to call off biker toy runs since the last one led to the shootout and threats to law enforcement! Stop allowing the gangs charity events to create a way to fool the public and recruit members.
>
> —from a Wise County, Texas,
> news site's letter to the editor, May 2015

> It is getting the time of year again for the annual obnoxious Toy Run, with its ear-splitting noise and no help from local law enforcement, even though the noise is totally illegal.
> For years now, I have asked our local law enforcement, including the state police, why we, as taxpayers, have to put up with this obnoxious noise.
>
> —Comment to a Maine newspaper, September 2013

So, toy runs are really recruitment recons, and only non-bikers in Maine pay taxes? There's a couple of mysteries—and maybe a myth or two—unto themselves.

Now, let's hear some of law enforcement's "Bah, Humbugs!"

Infamous undercover infiltrator Jay Dobyns has been quoted as saying, "I think, as a society, and to a large extent even in law enforcement, we fall into the sense that these guys are these big, rough-looking teddy bears that do blood drives and toys runs and are harmless. The reality of it is that it's a very dangerous world, inhabited by violent men."

A 2010 "law enforcement–sensitive" special report on gangs from the RMIN (Rocky Mountain Information Network) gives us this opinion: "People must realize that OMGs are not a bunch of fun-loving, toy-toting good guys delivering gifts to needy kids. The investigations are staggering and go on and on. The incidents, beginning with Hollister, go on through the years and have shaped our image of the OMG culture, and no amount of spin, public relations, or veneer should make a bit of difference in exposing what the gangs stand for. Schmoozing the public has provided OMGs with an improved image, taking the spotlight off the terror and horror they mete out and overriding the malicious side of their culture."

Violent, spin, veneer, terror, horror, malicious. The sentiments of Dobyns and the Mile-High LEOs (Law Enforcement Officers) are not isolated; they are common throughout their industry. But there has to be another side, doesn't there?

MORALLY MAULING THOSE TRANSVESTITES

In the shining spirit (Christmas or otherwise) of fairness, law enforcement motorcycle clubs put on many hefty toy runs of their own. And off- and on-duty cops serve as escorts for many of the "secular" runs. That's all fine and dandy, but more and more, toy runs are becoming the media's and the cops' go-to example of MC shadiness and hypocrisy. They are often seen in the same dingy light as moral-mauling television preachers who get caught with transvestite hookers an hour after their latest "Send-Your-Savings-to-the-Savior-and-Me" telethon.

But do the behind-the-scenes mysteries, myths, and rumors negate the high dollars in sum-line totals that bikers bring to their communities? Even though, at times, those big bucks may be dumped on needy doorsteps by big "teddy bears" who in all rational reality are somewhere in between your kid's one-eyed softy and the extra-evil *Toy Story* villain-fluffster Lotso, rather than in the top-tier tumult of Jay Dobyns's "world of violent men"?

Always a toy-run favorite, strapped to sissy bar after sissy bar, Buzz Lightyear might just have the answer. He said something to lawman Woody in the first *Toy Story* that would be a kick to hear him repeat to Dobyns if the two ever sat down for a beer: "Sheriff, this is no time to panic."

TSF, FTS!

REACTION AND RESPONSE

Toy runs are indeed a big target for law enforcement, because—like back patches—they are high-profile and easy for detractors to aim at. But when organization after organization gets handed a chunky check or a truckload of toys for their charity, they seldom care if their benefactors look—and act—more like a "big, rough-looking teddy bear" than clean-cut Ken on Barbie's pink-and-purple Glam Scooter. It's a hard-bottom line to ignore—but, still, many do.

CHAPTER 16:

SWINGIN' IN THE WIND WITH THE LYNCH REPORT

THE LOONIEST LEGAL DOCUMENT EVER?

INTERROGATING THE SUBJECT

Does the Lynch Report represent the first official governmental volley in the war between authorities and bikers?

The 1954 movie *The Wild One* was a slice-of-seedy-life picture about a pack of
vicious, swaggering motorcycle hoods called the Black Rebels. The characters
were too overdrawn and the violence they wrought was too unrelieved to
engage the credulity of its audience, so the film passed quickly into oblivion.
Last week it was back—in real life. The story was told by California Attorney
General Thomas C. Lynch, in a shocking report on a motorcycle gang....

—*Time* magazine, Friday March 26, 1965

Time obviously had its journalistic head stuffed pretty far up its center spread with
the comments about *The Wild One* having "passed quickly into oblivion." They
were, however, right on the money in calling the Lynch Report "shocking."

But, as expressed by Inigo Montoya in *The Princess Bride*, "You keep using
that word. I do not think it means what you think it means." *Time* meant "shocking"
in the sense that it supposedly exposed real and up-close animals to a shuddering world
that had spent the prior dozen years fear-frozen by the media. Movies such as *One Way
Ticket to Hell*, *Dragstrip Riot*, and the creepy short film *Scorpio Rising* put bad 'cycle guys
and delinquents on early '60s drive-in screens and in exploratory art theaters. The Lynch
Report put them directly on top of their daughters.

The report was *really* shocking—when that word means what we now know it
means—in two ways: one was that it was the first time a sanctioned governmental anti-
biker dispatch was issued; and second, sections of it read like an underground comic book.

HEAVY REACTION TO "HOODLUM ACTIVITIES"

The fairly short, fifteen-page condemnation of everything biker was the creative account
of the Honorable Thomas Conner Lynch, Attorney General of the State of California
from 1964 to 1971. His "tactical information" about "disreputable motorcycle riders"
was released to the state's Department of Justice on March 15, 1965, and was in response
to some well-publicized crimes alleged to have been committed by club members. But
its over-heavy reaction was like killing a fly on your living room plate-glass window by
throwing a brick at it.

> The Lynch Report, as it has come to be known, can be seen as the
> first large-scale bureaucratic attempt to portray motorcycle clubs as a
> clear and present danger to local, state, and ultimately international
> constituencies. The report consists of what can be interpreted as
> little more than urban legends: unsubstantiated absurdities such
> as gang raping of innocent young women and the plundering of

small California townships, all of which fall under the heading of "Hoodlum Activities."

—Arthur Veno, *The Mammoth Book of Bikers*

But Lynch's legends and absurdities became "real life" to *Time*, and the New York mag wasn't alone. The *Los Angeles Times*, *The New York Times*, *Newsweek*, *The Nation*, *Life*, and the *Saturday Evening Post* all jumped on Tom's tip-off train, and article after article spread his sensationalistic screeds.

Probably the most universal common denominator in identification of [club members] is their generally filthy condition. Investigating officers consistently report these people, both club members and their female associates, seem badly in need of a bath.

—the Lynch Report

Lynch was distributing his report to law enforcement agencies throughout the state, asking for feedback and a sharing of any additional information. He was clearly engineering a crackdown that he hoped would lead to further legal troubles for the clubs. That, coupled with the mainstream press running with Lynch's scare-stories and allegations, was a rich recipe for the legislation of many future motorcyclist-specific laws.

It's apparent now, in this era of RICO-replays and property seizures, that the mix was cooked-up to perfection.

LYNCH THE PRESIDENT?

Over the years, the attorney general's scoops have been branded by researchers as being "largely fiction compiled from questionable police files." But it doesn't matter. What the Lynch Report once again proves is that the biker image—whether true or fabricated— remains one of the strongest, most enduring, and most polarizing in American culture.

And it will forever produce strong, enduring, and polarizing reactions.

In 1968, Thomas Lynch actually made a run for the presidency of the United States. No one remembers that.

Nor do they remember much about his tenure as Cali's top cop—other than that report.

It's a document that remains relevant because it was the opening Looney Tunes theme that kicked off the endless Sylvester-Tweety/Roadrunner-Coyote chase-downs between badges and bikers. Hollister may have paced off the feud, but Thomas C. Lynch made it policy-official.

STILL HAUNTING AFTER ALL THESE YEARS

The 2014 American Heroes Channel series *Codes and Conspiracies* featured a segment titled "The Lynch Report Haunts Motorcycle Clubs." One of the experts interviewed was college professor, biker, and author William Dulaney.

"The Lynch Report tattooed on the American psyche the outlaw biker image that just will not die," Dulaney stated, reemphasizing the immortality of the aura. "That die that was cast in the '60s for the bikers, that mold is still alive and well today, and that's pretty much how America sees them."

And apparently always will.

Wherever the spirit of Thomas Lynch may be today, it's a safe bet that he's pleased with the timelessness of that mold—a mold that's not going anywhere anytime soon because, of course, bikers perpetually "seem badly in need of a bath."

REACTION AND RESPONSE

The Lynch Report was absolutely the first bureaucratically born and bred biker blast—just the thing to change simple public apprehension into a long-running litany of hard and limiting laws.

CHAPTER 17:

MIND GAMES

INSIDE THE SNITCH'S SUBCONSCIOUS

INTERROGATING THE SUBJECT
Do snitches really think about what they do?

Some are cops.
Some are mercenaries.
Some are out for personal vengeance.
All are hated.

One of the main reasons for the prospect period in a motorcycle club is to really, really, really get to know a potential brother from the inside out—and that includes finding out if he's a cop, a liar, a snitch, or all of the above.

But sometimes, even with background checks, lie-detector tests, sponsorship from respected members, and other ferreting feats, one or all the above can fall through some pretty thin cracks. And thin is all it takes, because even when they slither through the narrowest of openings, they take with them info, recordings, secretly-snapped pics, and club business that—when spun in a variety of ways—can give authorities the kind of takedown ammo they dream about during night sweats.

THE SCOURGE OF THE SCOOTERIZED STOCKHOLM SYNDROME

The crass common denominator among virtually all infiltrators is that they turn their aberrant adventures into high-stepping media marches. There they are on TV, shrouded in shadows with voice distortion on inner-gang-secrets-exposed cable shows. They are onstage, lecturing at law enforcement seminars. They become consultants for the police and other legal legions.

And they write books.

And that's usually the place where the between-the-lines psyches are laid the most bare. That's the place—especially with undercover cops—where you can see a shared slipping into a strange kind of scooterized Stockholm Syndrome, where they grow to prefer their biker brotherhood to that of their badged buddies.

Three of the most infamous undercover-infiltrator-snitch-authors of all time are predicament-perfect examples, having wrestled extensively with the chokehold of "capture bonding."

"BILLY"

Arguably still number one on the "snitches are a dying breed" chart is William Queen, a now-retired second-generation ATF agent, policeman, and Border Patrol agent. But his 2005 publication, *Under and Alone: The True Story of the Undercover Agent Who Infiltrated America's Most Violent Outlaw Motorcycle Gang*, is riddled with cops-versus-club conscience-conflicts.

> I grabbed the [club's] top rocker and waved it like a precious flag. A genuine sense of pride welled up inside of me.... I wanted that patch for real—Jesus, I had made it!...I was a fully patched-in member of the most violent outlaw motorcycle gang in America!... I was doing ninety miles per hour and feeling sky-high.... Nothing else mattered. I'd fucking done it....
>
> Living full-time as an outlaw gave me a perspective few law-enforcement officers ever get to experience. I was often more at risk from my supposed brothers in blue than from my adopted brothers in the gang. Just as there were some decent qualities—loyalty, love, respect—among the outlaw bikers, there were some law-enforcement officers who were little more than outlaws with badges....
>
> By this time, I felt more welcome in the company of these one-percenters than I did among my fellow law-enforcement officers. I wanted to be at [the bar] on this warm night, wanted to have a beer with the L.A. members, and the thought of persecuting any of them was not in my mind....
>
> When my mom died and no one from ATF had so much as offered their condolences, but the whole of the [club] embraced me...and told me, "I love you, Billy," I felt and understood the bond holding together these outlaw motorcycle gangs....
>
> We could take down their gun-trafficking networks, bust their drug-dealing operations, prosecute them for extortion and armed robbery and rape and homicide. The thing we could never attack was the love these guys felt for their brothers; in many cases it was a love stronger than for their blood relations. It was stronger than the most addictive narcotic.

"JAYBIRD"

Another now-retired Special Agent and ATFer, Jay Anthony "Jaybird" Dobyns, rode to infiltrator-infamy between 2004 and 2009 with his involvement in the feds' Operation Black Biscuit, his subsequent book about the undercover affair, and a strange lawsuit he initiated—and eventually won—against all of his LEO pals.

It seems that after the 2004 Operation Black Biscuit trials—trials that didn't quite produce as much destruction for the club Dobyns infiltrated as the ATF had hoped—the feds withdrew their "backstopping" protection, exposing Dobyns and his family to threats and actual violence. Things became very uncomfortable in Undercoverville.

But along the bumpy way, Dobyns, too, managed to feel some of the warmth from the biker brotherhood he was attempting to break.

> Bobby hugged us too. As he finished with me he grabbed my shoulders and said, "Remember, Bird—a [club member] may not always be right, but he is always your brother."
>
> Teddy spoke again. "Half of what's mine is yours. Don't forget that either."
>
> Their words made sense. Even though I'd sworn an oath to fight guys like these, I'd bought into some of their credo. I knew that any of these guys, and more than a few others across the state, would gladly take a bullet for me. In that instant I believed in some of what [the club] stood for. I was genuinely touched . . . as we've seen, things aren't always so cut-and-dried. I went in deep and realized that the [club members] weren't all bad—and I wasn't all good.

"CONTRACTED AGENT" CAINE

Alex Caine wasn't a cop; he was a mercenary—er, sorry, a "contracted agent" (as he puts it)—selling his services to various agencies. He, too, is now retired from the Lord's legal work, but not before having infiltrated international mobs, the KKK, and some of the biggest MCs on earth. In sheer numbers of operations, he may be the slipperiest crack-slipper of all.

The title of his first book, 2008's *Befriend and Betray*, straight-up says it all about what a mercenary does. It's simple and it's cold. But again, no matter how tough, experienced, and hardened an infiltrator may be, the beacon of biker brotherhood can shine through it all and generate at least a little hot passion within the snitch's icy underground.

Serious words of warning.

The more I got to know [the club I was infiltrating], the more
fascinated I became with them.... Like me...they had almost all
served in Vietnam.... [they] had been formed by disenchanted,
recently discharged vets.... In this way, I discovered, I had just as
much of a bond with most of [the club members] as I did with the
cops. More, in fact, if you took into account my delinquent youth.

Caine's "bond" with the cops got even looser at the end of one particular operation,
an operation that spurred his retirement. Not only did he get little recognition for the
work he had done—considered an outsider, not an official bona fide law enforcement
officer—but the protect-and-serve agency wound up screwing him over, big time, by
destroying much of his personal property.

That gesture helped to convince me that getting out of the game,
one I'd been playing on and off for a quarter century, was the right
idea. Infiltration is hard enough when you know who your friends
are; when you don't know if the cops will stand behind you or what
their real agenda is, well, there are better ways to make a living.

NOT-SO-HAPPILY EVER AFTER

But even with all of the temporary softening, flash epiphanies, and who's-really-got-
your-back revelations, in the end, every one of the infiltrators ultimately answered the
voices in their head that backed the badge.

Their personal and occupational rewards for that choice, however, appear
to be varied.

Queen's operation, aided by another seven hundred LEO in four states, led to the
convictions on various charges of fifty-three people. Dobyns's operation, judging by his
legal battles with his own kind, was a disaster. Caine's many forays have brought varying
judicial results, but his final distrust of the cops must be troubling for him.

AVENGING AXES AND DEMON REPENTANCE

In addition to the infiltrators who have purposely gone deep for the law are snitchers
of other stripes who simply seem to arise. Pissed-off ex-club members with an avenging
axe to grind; or those who are all-in but suddenly "repent" and must cast off the
demons they once called brothers. And while not enduring mind games as intense as the
covert cops, they still must suffer a sleepless night or two as they accuse, allege, testify,
and hide.

The odd enigma that is Edward Winterhalder is one of those former club members.
His first book, a four-hundred-plus-page epic, is ostensibly a tell-all about a major club

that bounced him. But it's a little hard to get there as the reader wades through every single minute detail of Winterhalder's life, essentially from the time he was born—including such important facts as where he went to kindergarten. That kind of thing on your literary résumé is, in itself, a reason for some tossing and turning.

But Ed may actually sleep fairly well when it comes to any guilt about his exposé. He analyzes his former club with the same kind of political probing as a *New York Times* editorial around election time. He comes to a very heady conclusion that all the MC's negatives were brought about by poor leadership—that the club's former president "somehow forgot his values and ideals, and lost his integrity along the way, rather than guiding the club non-traditionally as he initially set out to do."

Then Winterhalder ties his entire study to the old cliché about "absolute power corrupting," and optimistically adds that the MC will learn from its experiences and "probably live on forever."

Good night and pleasant dreams.

Another spiller of secrets who "simply seemed to arise"—and then fall—was George Wethern. Unfortunately for him, George didn't have quite the same calculating political outlook on things that Winterhalder had.

Wethern's 1978 book, *A Wayward Angel* (which is still included in many scholars' and researchers' "must read" biker bibliographies), was a pioneer of the repentance crowd. Drugs were his demon:

> I know quite a bit about drugs through my own stupidity, but I think I can turn it around to help other people. If some of the damn drugs can be stopped through my efforts, maybe some of the killings will stop. If what I'm going to tell saves one life, it'll be worth it....

And apparently *he* thought a lot about what he was doing. After testifying in court against former brothers, Wethern and his wife disappeared into a witness protection program.

MIND GAMES IN THE MUCK

Other flailing arms of the infiltrator/snitch syndicate include the ghostwriters, the "with" writers, and the outside investigators who step into that media march, working the words and wills of the whistle-blowers. Where the mind games and subconscious slides come in here is twofold: How can these writers clear their own consciences as they type up what they hope will be the bring-down of an entire club and possibly the whole lifestyle; something most of them have never been a part of? And how can the snitch/infiltrators look at the finished product—often wacky and excessive—be proud of it, and pray for a Pulitzer?

One of the more notorious outside writers is Canadian Yves Lavigne, who has written with a lustful fire about one of the more notorious snitches, Anthony Tait. Together they are quite the pair. Lavigne has penned a damning library of writings with destruction and negativity in every word. Tait wallows in the same muck.

> The real sad part with Dobyns and William Queen, both making statements that they sincerely liked many members and felt close to the clubs they infiltrated. . . . Not Tait though. Of all the infiltrators, rats, informants, and people who turn or flip, he was out to fuck everyone he could for the benefit of Anthony Tait.
>
> —nicatic.com

The answer to how Lavigne keeps his conscience clear may be that he's just as narcissistic as Tait; in this case a self-set shrink with miraculous interpretive powers:

> I realized then that I would have to get further into Anthony Tait's head than anyone had been to understand the drives that propelled him into the underworld and then into the arms of law enforcement to sell out his fellow bikers.

Spinning mind games of his own, with a single-focus crusade of dismantling the MC culture—that is the inner workings of Yves Lavigne:

> Bleeding hearts and rednecks consider [motorcycle club members] the last truly free men—those who dare break laws. It is a sorry myth bred in ignorance and man's willingness to smother in fantasy rather than chase his visions.
> The myth must die.

SOP: SUNKEN EYES AND THE STENCH OF URINE

In the wackiness and excess department, "with" writer Kerrie Droban's mega-melodramatic look at the biker culture screams with myth, mystery, and rumor. She now has several biker books in her "with" pile of infiltration-exposés.

While her spinning moral compass might not be as pointed as those she writes with, she shows rather obviously what she thinks about things. The energetic way in which she portrays the various lairs in the biker jungle makes for quite the scene-setting.

And fun.

First there's the constant decay and disgusting odors.

Every clubhouse, or really every place bikers meet, is dark, dank, and smelly: "With the stench of urine lingering in the air…his team parked in front of the clubhouse dump that resembled a small prison barracks.…Negotiations with transactions occurred sometimes at three and four o'clock in the morning in smelly cars.…"

Then there are the eyes.

The next time you're around bikers, check if they have "sunken eyes" or "eyes narrowed to slits" or eyes like "pellets"? Do they have "eyes that were skittish"? Do they have "eyes like chips, veined and scratchy as if dried too long in the sun"?

The bikers Ms. Droban describes do.

Take another look around.

Check the overall expression of the nearest biker. Does he have a look "like a spider, his smile tight and forced, his gaze menacing and accusatory"?

The bikers that Ms. Droban describes have this special look; a look that she and other "with" writers feel that bikers are supposed to have.

Scene after scene is word-painted like a Halloween party in an abandoned, crumbling asylum.

And maybe that would be a real hoot—if the guest list were to include undercover law enforcement officers, mercenaries, angry ex-clubbers, outlaws-in-rehab, cub-reporter crusaders, investigative zealots, and interpretive ghosts. Then, at midnight, they could all urinate on the already-smelly floor, narrow their spider-chip eyes, and share their tales of snitchery and deceit.

REACTION AND RESPONSE

Hell, yes, snitches think about what they do! Some agonize over where their loyalties really lie. Some suffer regret about where their lives have led them and are trying to make amends. Some think about the opportunity—legal or otherwise—that being a part of the betrayal buys them. Some are cold and narcissistic, thinking only of their own glory. But, consciously or subconsciously, all are aware of the power of this lifestyle and how turning against it can change one's life forever.

CHAPTER 18:

THE PARADOX OF THE PIGS

CLUB CUTS WITH A BADGE IN THE POCKET

INTERROGATING THE SUBJECT

Which came first, the biker or the bacon? And hey, why do so many law
enforcement clubs adopt the same image—and just about everything else—as
one-percenter MCs? Oh, and one more thing: how's that working out for them?

L aw enforcement officers (LEOs) are not welcome in virtually any major MC, one-percenter or otherwise.

Period.

A question is quickly asked of every hangaround. It goes something like: "Are you now or have you ever been involved in law enforcement?"

There is only one answer that will work.

It is a rock-hard and furiously fast rule that does not bend, because the two factions do not blend. It's the simple difference between staid living and rebellion. Between cautious control and reckless fun-fueled freedom. What we're talking here is the difference between snake and mongoose DNA. Killer venom versus razor teeth.

And because of that stinging separation, down through the years law enforcement has done its best to try and put the clubs out of business. They have infiltrated, infuriated, and excoriated them. They have used RICO in attempts to reduce their ranks. They have seized their intellectual property. They have used decibel meters, handlebar heights, turn-signal placements, mirror sizes, emission-cans, and myriad mechanical minutiae to neuter their bikes.

They are the enemy and no one is going to invite their enemy to their party.

"Keep your friends close and your enemies closer" may work in politics and soap operas, but it doesn't work among people who are supposed to be your "brothers."

"HOW LOW CAN YOU GO?"

So what happens to cops who ride? What happens to cops who are in that awkward limbo of enjoying an in-the-wind wildness while living an oath-committed, sin-light existence, free of legal "association" with what RICO refers to as the "enterprise" of OMGs?

They start their own MCs.

And there's a zillion of them.

Many have even embraced the "pig" term by using it in the names of their clubs; a squealing twist on some outlaw clubs' "fuck you" acceptance of the one-percenter brand.

Formally, many are known as Public Safety and Law Enforcement Motorcycle Clubs. The "public safety" clause has been added because firefighters, paramedics, and other badged public servants have comingled with police in these clubs. Still, overall, the MC world refers to them simply as "cop clubs." And the organizations that are limited strictly to LEOs are the biggest enigma; with many blue levels of myths, mysteries, and rumors.

COP BY DAY, BIKER BY NIGHT

Their own brothers of the shield fear the worst in LEO MCs. They are skeptical, skittish, and suspect pseudo-schizophrenia in their "brothers'" newfound lifestyle leanings!

> An increasing number of police officers are forming motorcycle clubs, and hundreds now exist nationwide, according to experts on motorcycle gangs. Gang investigators fear that such clubs, some of which have the trappings of outlaw biker groups, can hurt the credibility of law enforcement and undermine criminal cases brought against traditional gangs.
>
> "In the last 15 years, I would say that we've probably seen a tenfold increase in these clubs," said Terry Katz, vice president of the International Outlaw Motorcycle Gang Investigators Association, who works for the Maryland State Police. "The first ones were pretty straightforward. They were family-oriented clubs. What we see now as a trend is biker by night and cop by day."
>
> —Cyril Huze Post, July 24, 2013

And the hits just keep a-comin'. A 2015 Associated Press article turns up the volume on the internal affairs antagonism, a struggle that gets louder and clearer with every instance of interaction instead of incarceration:

> Concord, N.H.—Police officers and outlaw biker gangs often stand on common ground. Both attract the young and adventurous who value order, discipline and brotherhood. And on weekends tens of thousands of cops routinely trade their cruisers and badges for choppers and club colors....
>
> The bond doesn't mean a free pass for criminal motorcycle gangs, but even some within law enforcement worry that too many officers believe bikers are just misunderstood Robin Hoods. And empathy from officers who emulate or even aspire to the outlaw life can put police or the public at risk, gang experts warn....
>
> "They're supposed to be putting them in jail, not schmoozing with them, not socializing with them," said Charlie Fuller, a retired special agent with the federal Bureau of Alcohol, Tobacco, Firearms and Explosives. "That's a no-brainer to me. You have a

huge security issue for the whole department. Here's a cop that's hanging with them socially. What's he telling them? What are they asking him...?"

A 2014 ATF report said biker gangs count working police officers, firefighters and 911 workers as members.... Laconia police Chief Chris Adams, whose New Hampshire town will attract hundreds of thousands of bikers to its annual Motorcycle Week starting on June 13, said he has seen some officers instantly transform when they're wearing club colors instead of their uniform.

"Some of them won't look at you or talk to you," Adams said. He called the fuzzy lines between police and bikers a "valid concern...."

Steve Cook, who leads the Midwest Outlaw Motorcycle Gang Investigators Association, says some of the legit [cop] clubs go to "totally embarrassing" lengths to ingratiate themselves to criminal gangs.

"They're going to a 1-percent gang and asking permission to start their club up," he said. "You've got to pick a side. You're either a cop or a biker."

But the very existence of law enforcement clubs can stoke violence, Fuller said:

"They want to be like them, but not them," Fuller said of the law enforcement clubs. "It agitates the real 1-percenters that cops want to come and imitate them at all."

Jay Dobyns, a former undercover agent who infiltrated [a major MC] for the ATF, worries that chumminess between biker gangs and the more benign law enforcement motorcycle clubs can lead to a perception that cops will go easy on the outlaws.

When Dobyns was undercover, he said, cops from motorcycle clubs would try to cozy up to the outlaw bikers.

"I'm talking about the clean-cut law enforcement officers who wear a uniform and ride around in marked cruisers every day; then Saturday comes around and they put on a black bandanna and black T-shirt and scowl at everybody," he said.

The gang members were having none of it.

"'We're never going to be friends,'" was how "true believers" in the bike gang reacted to such interlopers, Dobyns said. "Some of these cop clubs don't get that."

—Associated Press, June 7, 2015

UNINVITED NEIGHBORS

Observers of military members' involvement with OMGs agree with Dobyns that LEO clubs aren't exactly in favor with the three-piece-patch clubs they are sworn to persecute but then try to emulate. And that may present them with a much harsher foe than their strait-laced brother cops and pissed-off chiefs and commissioners.

> In southern and central Maryland, [a major one-percent MC] is furious that the Iron Order [an LEO MC] continues to don a three-piece patch. In the past 2 months, there have been several bloody confrontations between the two. On February 28, 2014, both were involved in a melee at a strip club in Baltimore. [The major MC] members were equipped with bats, knives, MagLite flashlights and hammers. Even though nobody was killed, both OMGs suffered major injuries.
>
> One week later, as three Iron Order members were idling at a red light in Prince George's County, they were viciously attacked by several car loads of suspected [major MC] members. Two of the three Iron Order members were severely beaten with bats, ax handles and crow bars. The assailants were not wearing colors or indicia that depicted they were [major MC] members, supporters or associates. [Analyst Note: The Iron Order is one of the fastest growing motorcycle clubs in the United States. Members wear a traditional three-piece patch with a State bottom rocker. The fact that they wear the State bottom rocker has infuriated the [major MCs in their area]. More importantly, many of their members are police and corrections officers, active-duty military and/or government employees and contractors. Over the past 4 years, the Iron Order has had several violent confrontations with [OMGs]. Per the Texas Department of Public Safety (DPS), in 2013, an Iron Order member was run off the road by a [major MC] member. In Clarksville, Kentucky, the Iron Order and [another major MC] have been involved in several violent altercations. On May 14, 2011, [another major MC] member...stabbed an Iron Order member outside a bar in South Carolina. Despite the violence, they continue to move into territory controlled by one of the Dominant 7.]
>
> —*OMGs and the Military 2014*, ATF Report

Even undercover snitches like Dobyns himself can smell hyper-hypocrisy; especially when it reeks and rots with double-standards and duplicity.

> We came across a group of bikers who called themselves the Wild Pigs. One of their guys walked up to us, his hand extended to meet Bobby. He wore a big shit-eating smile. He said, "Hey, pleasure to meet you."
>
> Bobby raised his sunglasses and looked at him intently. He did not offer his hand in return. "Get fucked."
>
> "Hey, I—"
>
> "You heard me, fuck off. Can you believe these cocksuckers, Bird?" I didn't lie—I said no, I couldn't. The Wild Pigs were cops, guys with badges who paraded around on weekends like a One-Percenter club. In my mind, as in Bobby's, they were a fucking abomination.
>
> The guy took his hand back and started to turn when Bobby said, "Wait. I gotta tell you something—you can't have it both ways, asshole. You can't pretend to look and act like us until the shit gets nasty and then pull a badge and gun and sit us down on the side of the road. Fuck you. Pick a side." He turned away in disgust and flipped the Wild Pig off. I followed him. Bobby couldn't have been more right. It was one thing to be undercover. It was another to be flying two flags at once.
>
> —Jay Dobyns, *No Angel*

PRAISE THE LARD AND PASS THE RAMIFICATIONS

Karen Katz's 2011 book *Behind the Patch: Towards an Understanding of Public Safety and Law Enforcement Motorcycle Clubs*, highlights a third poison poke for the pigs; and that is from within their own inter- and intra-club ranks—a situation that the media love to exploit when it comes to similar issues involving one-percenters. But, darn, it just seems out of cop-character for the LEO clubs.

Karen chronicles the long and complex, yes, *trademark*-rights mud-match and brotherhood-bash that split Jay Dobyns's acquaintances in the Wild Pigs into a sooey-sized platter of boneless pork chops. According to Karen, inner-Pig wrangling led to—in one way or another—the establishment of LEO MCs that included the Warthogs, Iron Pigs, Punishers, Iron Warriors, Gunfighters, Renegade Pigs, Untouchables, Guardians, and Gatekeepers.

So, in time, everything turned out hunky-dory, it seems. And Karen softened the badged brotherhood blow-up by saying that "Outlaw bikers would have enforced their own code to deal with the conflicts. For example, problem members would have been severely beaten or murdered."

That may have been a bit of overreaching conjecture, but she is right about outlaw bikers having codes.

But so do cops.

Upheld by the ranks of law enforcement is the well-recognized but unwritten code known as "the blue wall of silence," "blue code," or "blue shield."

And its "enforcement" can have ramifications for those within the LEO tribe and the outside citizenry as well.

> The Blue Code of Silence is an unwritten rule among police officers in the U.S. not to report on the errors, misconducts or crimes of one of their fellow officers. According to the unwritten code, if an officer is questioned about an incident of misconduct involving another officer, the officer being questioned will claim to be unaware of another officer's wrongdoing.... The term "whistleblower" comes to mind, when being used to describe someone who breaks the unwritten blue code.... Many officers fail to challenge the blue code, because doing so could mean they are challenging long-standing traditions and feelings of brotherhood within the law enforcement family.... One of the other primary reasons that officers choose to follow the blue code and keep their mouths shut, is because they fear facing the consequences that come as a result of it....
> —*Houston Forward Times*, September 10, 2014

A 2000 conference of the International Association of Chiefs of Police exposed the results of a study about the "code." In between what was undoubtedly a rip-roaring weekend of wildness, twenty-five basic law enforcement academies from over a dozen states researched, administered, and collected over a thousand confidential questionnaires completed by academy recruits. The findings confirmed the code:

- 79% said that a law enforcement Code of Silence exists and is fairly common throughout the nation.

- 52% said that the fact a Code of Silence exists doesn't really bother them.

- 24% said the Code of Silence is more justified when excessive force involves a citizen who's abusive.

- 46% said they would not tell on another officer for having sex on duty.

- 23% said they wouldn't tell on another cop for regularly smoking marijuana off duty.

The study produces many conclusions, but one in particular was interesting—and a little frightening: because the code is an essentially natural occurrence, attempts to stop it all together will be futile.

NO SECOND CHANCE TO MAKE A BAD IMPERSONATION

There is, however, a hard-written code that lays out one more enigma—and one more inequity—of police officers putting on the persona of one-percenters. It's a law, actually, and it's federal and recognized in every state. California's version goes like this:

> *California Penal Code Section 538d. (a)*
> Any person other than one who by law is given the authority of a
> peace officer, who willfully wears, exhibits, or uses the authorized
> uniform, insignia, emblem, device, label, certificate, card, or writing,
> of a peace officer, with the intent of fraudulently impersonating a
> peace officer, or of fraudulently inducing the belief that he or she is a
> peace officer, is guilty of a misdemeanor.

Obviously, no such law exists for impersonating a biker.

REACTION AND RESPONSE

Okay, maybe a guy got into bikes before he pinned on his badge, or even afterward. But the heavy social action of becoming a law officer changes many things—including one's lifestyle. The Lynch Report set the tone; subsequent laws and legal actions set the crusade. For good or ill, cops and MCs are an uncomfortable mix. "You can't have it both ways" are words of wisdom that can be applied to many parts of life, but they are especially potent here.

CHAPTER 19:

SEMINAR SECRETS

WHAT "THEY" ARE BEING TAUGHT ABOUT "US"

INTERROGATING THE SUBJECT

Okay, we've combed through all the goofy old and new LEO training manuals about OMGs, but has anyone from the cop-inside ever opened up about closed-door trainings, dedicated "biker investigators," and other specialized drills?

Then there was instruction regarding traffic stops of bikers. The information indicated that stopping bikers on a run was a potential powder keg. It was actually stated that in assessing what you (the officer) have stopped, "If it looks like a biker and smells like a biker, you've stopped a biker." Imagine if that comment was applied to a group officially recognized as a minority!

—From the beans-spilling statements of an LEO
who wishes to remain anonymous

Nationwide, gang investigative organizations and associations are everywhere. A big part of what they do is to have seminars, lots of seminars. Huge sharings of information about everything gang: from tattoos to graffiti to hand signs to ethnic histories to cartel capers to pants-on-the-ground—the whole steaming enchilada.

But one seminar subject is sacred.

One seminar subject is highly and selectively screened.

One seminar subject is for special eyes and ears only.

All the other agenda item classes can be attended by a wide mix: "sworn federal, state, local or tribal law enforcement officers; correctional officers; intelligence analysts; prosecutors; investigators for prosecutors currently employed by an agency or department; parole and probation officers; Military Police; criminal justice professionals"; a variety of others in differing parts of the legal biz, and sometimes even concerned citizens.

But the hardcore examinations of OMGs? They are not for just anyone.

EXPOSING THE TERRIBLE TRUTH ABOUT MANDATORY RIDES

The International Outlaw Motorcycle Gang Investigators Association (IOMGIA) is one of the heaviest hitters among those poke-and-prod bodies, and they are one hundred percent about OMGs. Their seminar restrictions say it all about this subject's exclusivity and wide-open "We Reserve the Right to Refuse Service to Anyone" attitude that dogs it:

IOMGIA will not allow attendance or membership to persons deemed to be involved in conduct off-duty that is unbecoming or contrary to the stated goals of the association. This includes membership in motorcycle clubs that mimic the structure and/or nature of outlaw motorcycle gangs to include:

• Wearing three-piece patches
• Requiring a probationary period for membership
• Mandatory rides

Huh? That third "involvement" is especially curious. When did "mandatory rides" make one an outlaw, unbecoming, or contrary?

We may not be able to unravel a mystery *that* monstrous and murky, but we can certainly dig into plenty of other myths and rumors about what "they" are being told about "us."

SPILLING THE BLUE BEANS

Just as some snitches and infiltrators have slipped through tiny cracks in MCs' prospecting probes, occasionally it happens on the flipside as well. Not that he's either, but recently a veteran law enforcement officer and investigator peeled back all that goes on in those sealed-seminars and in other areas of official discussion, blue behavior, and education concerning OMGs.

The guy rides, has a conscience, appreciates the truth, and pours out the best and most complete inside commentary on this sacred subject ever spilled.

Here are his thoughts from the blue inside:

> I'm a retired cop from a large state police agency with the bulk of my career (thirty years) spent in the SWAT and drug enforcement arena. The other side of the coin is that I've been riding for quite a while and am a member of a motorcycle club for high-risk military and law enforcement—i.e., Delta, SWAT, etc. From the "insider's" perspective, it is amazing the great amount of disinformation and out-and-out bullshit generated about bikers in the world of law enforcement intelligence.
>
> However, since I still have some contact with my old agency—most importantly, the annual retiree qualification shoot since the state I live in is ass-backward regarding concealed carry for private citizens—I thought it best to go the anonymous route. I hate to "wimp out" like that, but I still teach around the country and my department could blackball me if they chose to. I'd hate to lose my fun-money source which pays for motorcycle toys and trips. While I don't entirely trust state government, I trust the feds even less.
>
> So here we go...
>
> About police in general: if a cop is an asshole to the public, in many cases, the cops he/she works with can't stand him or her either. These types are usually assholes to everyone. Of course, there are some who just maintain a hard-on for particular groups, for God knows what personal reasons.

But so much of the hatred by cops for bikers is relatively simple: it's based on stereotypes. And so many of these stereotypes come from the bullshit intelligence bulletins put out about bikers—specifically 1%ers. Some of these bulletins and training materials are totally off the wall, but this is what forms the attitudes and behaviors of cops who don't know better, especially the newbies. New cops can be like probationary motorcycle club members; they're busting their ass to make a mark for themselves.

RERUN AFTER RERUN OF *THE BIG BANG THEORY*

Letting more cop-cats out of the bag, our insider expands on the stale "secrets" that live on and on and on.

So many of these intel publications use the fear element—warning cops of all those things that the higher-ups in law enforcement actually think that bikers commonly do. I know it's been covered again and again, but this one bears repeating for that specific reason: The old "shotgun-handlebars theory"—telling officers to be aware of the potential for bikers to rig a shotgun into the handlebars—is a mystery, myth, and rumor that will never die! It's a theory that's still alive—and living quite well.

One training aid actually had a photo of a motorcycle mirror, showing an officer walking up to the bike. The officer was reflected in the mirror with crosshairs on his head! Now, I realize that some folks are excellent machine fabricators and some are very innovative, but this always seemed just a bit far-fetched to me. I couldn't imagine what the configuration of the handlebars would be that would allow me to use my mirror for a sighting mechanism. In addition, if my handlebars/handgrips were so aligned that I could shoot someone behind me, I couldn't imagine how impractical it would be to ride that bike.

BEYOND BEATNIKING

It's always tough—and uncomfortable—when you have to sit and listen to something that you know is total BS. Especially when that BS is supposed to be greasing the wisdom wheels of your job, helping to make your work smooth and, above all, safe.

Another bit of information was that "most bikers carry extra keys and often install a special switch to bypass the ignition, requiring no key to start up and take off quickly!" Most? Really?

This seems to display pure ignorance, because as we well know, in the world of Harley, many models don't need a key as long as the ignition is unlocked. And sure, the FXRs that are considered the classic club bike don't have that option, but the extra key/bypass switch, cowboy-like, leaping, quick-mount escape was being passed off as the norm. I'm sure motor officers found this amusing.

Another training source actually did enlighten us in a positive sense by saying that present-day biker runs are no longer really like the movie *The Wild One*. I'm sure Stanley Kramer would be proud to know his work was still being used to frame the biker world some sixty-plus years after its release! I guess the message was that we cops no longer had to fear bikers showing up and talking like beatniks in a 1950s coffeehouse.

CREDIBILITY IS EVERYTHING

It's always confusing and conflicting when someone who has never really *done* something suddenly becomes an *expert* on that thing. Feathers on a bird-watcher don't make him an eagle...

Having supervised a covert narcotics unit and having been assigned to a DEA task force, I was always amused at all the cops who boasted themselves as "biker investigators" or some similar play on words. I truly believe that these guys thought that this made them "badder" than the average cop. In actuality, these guys were wannabe bikers in the worst way.

One particular investigator was considered to be our agency's "biker expert." He spoke at conferences, wrote articles, and the like. He maintained the appearance of the stereotypical biker, went to Sturgis every year—on company time—and the taxpayers' dime— did a lot of surveillance at various runs, etc. He taught all the cadet classes about the ins and outs of bikers.

After this man retired, he was coordinating training for local agencies in our area. I was also teaching for that entity, and during a break I asked him if he was getting much riding in. The man paused, and then sheepishly informed me that he never *did* ride. Just now, in retirement, he told me, he was learning how to ride a dirt bike with his son.

I was floored.

I couldn't figure how all the surveillance and undercover-bullshit stories I'd heard about this guy over the years could have been anything but fantasy. If there was any shred of truth to the information he'd passed down over the years, I'm sure it was lifted from some other agency's reports. At this point, there was zero credibility.

And credibility is everything.

A GREAT WAY TO FUCK OFF

If you've gone to even a few major runs or events, you've seen them: the law enforcement surveillance teams that park strategically, whip out binoculars and cameras, institute helicopter fly-bys, and "observe." But what really goes on behind *those* scenes?

A few years back, a well-known MC leader was at a local H-D shop for a book signing. I went to get my copy of the book signed and to meet the guy. Whatever people believe of his life, this man is a tremendous motivator and leader; after reading his books and meeting him twice, I wished we had folks like him running our department. Anyway, at the book signing, the local drug task force and "biker investigators" showed up and stood across the street taking copious photos and writing down license plate numbers. Funnier still were the "covert" cops wearing street clothes, bulletproof vests, and badges on chains around their necks. As a cop, I was fucking embarrassed for them. About halfway through the meet and greet, one of the cops sent over an emissary to purchase a club support shirt for him.

Back at the office on Monday, I ran into the DEA "biker investigator," who started giving me shit about being there. I responded by mentioning that he and his buddies looked like a bunch of stooges and asked why all these *Miami Vice* throwbacks gave away their "covert" identities and their covert cars by being so public.

His response was that they were trying to link and identify members of a smaller club who were in the process of patching over to the major MC in the area. I relished informing him that if his team had simply visited the website for the local MC's chapter, it showed pictures of them and the smaller club fraternizing—and that they had even gone through the trouble of identifying everyone by name below each photo. They could have saved a lot of government money by jumping on the Internet.

These biker investigators went to meeting after meeting and were *always* conducting surveillance. They *never* arrested anyone. I realized *I* was the dumbshit: here I was working for a living, while they had found a great way to fuck off.

"GO AHEAD, MAKE MY DAY!"

Our man on the inside next offered his thoughts about biker investigators and the OCDETF (Organized Crime Drug Enforcement Task Force—ad hoc task forces put together with federal monies thrown in to target a specific group or groups):

> Our SWAT team was tasked with gaining entry into a 1% clubhouse as a part of one of these investigations. We weren't involved in the investigation, but were the hired guns to make entry, secure the place, and turn it over to the investigators.
>
> Once we'd done our job, we stood on the perimeter and watched the investigators act like total assholes. They asked who had taken down (secured) one of the guys inside the clubhouse, and I responded that it was me—unsure what the issue was, as the man had been very compliant. Turns out they were laughing and making shit out of the guy because he'd pissed his pants. My response was that if *I'd* awoken in bed at six a.m. with a guy dressed in black pointing a submachine gun in my face, I'd probably piss my pants too.
>
> *If* there had been any trouble, *we'd* have had to deal with it. These assholes stood on the corner eating donuts, and when all was safe, they swaggered in like Dirty Harry.
>
> In this same raid, these guys' federal search warrant allowed them to seize anything with club- or motorcycle-related indicia on it. I witnessed them take a cardboard motorcycle shipping box with the H-D logo on it that a club member had gotten from the local shop to use as a wall decoration.
>
> Another embarrassing display.

LESSON ONE: WHY THEY PARK THAT WAY

Ever wonder why you park your bike with the ass-end against the curb? Well, wonder no more! Law enforcement has the answer!

> If you've watched any of the *Gangland* series on the History Channel, one particularly amusing episode is the one about the Galloping Goose MC. The cop who stars in this particular show, Steve Cook, is quite entertaining.

I taught a block at a national training conference where this same guy was teaching. On a break, I stepped into his class and pretty much pegged him for what I call a "drive-by" expert. That's a guy who has stood perimeter on a homicide scene or gone to a training class and is now qualified to teach homicide investigation. He said he was from a major Kansas City area department to make it sound like he was with KC Kansas or KCMO PD when he was actually with a Podunk suburb.

Anyway, in the Galloping Goose MC investigation, he and another cop went deep cover and tried to work into the club. They got Harleys and hung around, but no one would give them the time of day—he dresses this up a bit on the show. My favorite quote was when he stated that the club members would purposely park their bikes with the rear tire to the curb/clubhouse so law enforcement couldn't drive by and run their license plates.

I can see why his undercover ploy failed. Apparently he wasn't tuned in to the hazards of duck-walking a bike backwards into traffic if you park the thing in front first, or the extra challenges of doing so if the roadway is crowned—or the fact that it's required *by law* to park like that in many places. The bullshit-meters of the bikers he encountered probably went off as fast as the bullshit-meters of me and some of the other cops sitting in on his presentation.

REVISITING THE FIRM OF QUEEN, DOBYNS, AND CAINE

The "snitch's subconscious" is just as obvious to those on the inside as it is to those on the outside.

With respect to RICO and club prosecutions and other topics...here's my view—though perhaps not the average law enforcement opinion:

It seems there are distinct patterns in full-blown deep-cover/extended—read: extremely expensive—investigations: a large round-up with mass arrests, followed by just a handful of convictions on lesser charges for just a few club members. Of course, these deep-cover ops allow someone to play biker, live the lifestyle, and write books. This was true of Billy McQueen in *Under and Alone* and Jay Dobyns in *No Angel*.

In McQueen's book, he found his club "brothers" to be more considerate than his government brothers, and he experienced guilt over their arrests. Dobyns, too, enjoyed the lifestyle he was getting into.

From a law enforcement supervisor's viewpoint, you can identify the point in the book where his focus shifts from the investigation to patching into the club. Perhaps the most accurate account of Dobyns can be found in the book *Befriend and Betray*. The author, Alex Caine, is a mercenary-type informant. He crossed paths with Dobyns and paints a picture of the whole operation as being out of control. It's been a while since I've read this book, but as I recall, he indicated that the motorcycle clubs Dobyns was investigating were far better behaved than the group of cops in the undercover crash house in Laughlin, Nevada.

And the result? Like those damn shotgun handlebars, I know this has been covered, but I think it, too, bears repeating, especially from my perspective as a cop. So here it is: These operations seem to provide minuscule results for all the expense and grandiose visions.

In that Galloping Goose feature on *Gangland* ("Beware the Goose!"), the police ended up making cases against some of the members for drug dealing, through a very basic and inexpensive method. One: They sat up on a house they suspected of being a point of drug sales. Two: They stopped a "customer" for a traffic violation. Then, three, the customer agreed to turn informant. The case progressed from there. From a police perspective, the operation was deemed successful.

You would think at least a little futility would be seen in all of this—but the feds will continue to churn out their RICO and OCDETF cases with few results and little serious scrutiny.

Other things continue to churn as well.

SLOSHED AT THE SEMINARS

What *they* are being taught about *us* is not just done behind closed doors, it's the most secretive of all snoop-schooling.

The training sources and materials have expanded into huge seminars that focus on gangs in general and OMGs in particular—and it's interesting as to just how exclusive those OMG sessions are.

At an upcoming Gang Specialist Training Program in Chicago, for example, the agenda is huge, covering such topics as Asian Gangs, Female Gangs, Hate Group/White Supremacist Gangs, Gangs and the Mass Media, Gang/Extremist Groups in the Military—and Motorcycle Gangs.

This conference is open to "law-abiding individuals who have gathered to collect and share information about gangs and crime."

Except...

The only "training track" that is "restricted to Law Enforcement ONLY—as described in the event's flyer—is, of course, the one on "Motorcycle Gangs."

I just may attend that.

Ironically, some of my cop biker-wannabe thoughts are based on some of the guys who were assigned to me years ago when I was supervising a state task force. Every year an entity would host an OMG conference in the east central part of our state. This was a three-day training, which I believe was more of a three-day drunk—but hey, everyone needs some time away and the chance to let off steam. What was funny was that when the guys got back to the office, they plastered pictures of their trip by their desks. They were all dressed up in their biker best; it looked like a Halloween party. And a good number of these guys didn't own a motorcycle.

BADGE NO. 666

It seems like there was police "profiling" before it even had a name.

One of our retired troopers who came on the job in the 1960s was telling me that back in the day, he had to hide his Harley and the fact that he rode from the department. If his sergeant had found out, he would have been subject to dismal performance evaluations at best, and possibly some disciplinary action. The anti-biker hysteria was so strong that even one of the "good guys" must be bad if he swung his leg over a "motorsickle."

The trooper's name was Willis and I still run into him from time to time at the local Harley shop. He's pushing eighty, still rides, and puts on miles that would put many younger riders to shame. While one of the good guys, Willis seems to take special delight in that his department ID—badge—number was "666." I'm sure that if command back then had known of ol' Willy's biker tendencies, they would have seen him as "Wild Bill"—a renegade with a badge who redefined that "good guy" label very much in his own way.

DUDLEY DO-RIGHT VS. BILLY BAD-ASS

Our LEO exposé ends with some final ultra-perception about law enforcement clubs.

It's so very true that many of these groups want to go out and play badass biker and pretend to be 1%ers. The Wild Pigs are notorious for this. I've witnessed others, such as the Blue Knights, get involved in some really stupid (drunken) encounters with club members at some biker function when they decided they needed to play cop after a twelve-pack. Granted, this doesn't describe all of these groups' members, but I've sure seen this type of shit more than once. It's back to those inspiring words of wisdom again but most of these guys don't realize that they can't have it both ways. They can't be both Dudley Do-Right and Billy Badass.

Our club, with law enforcement members, maintains a "respect all" policy. We have a great relationship with our dominant local club, one of the Big Five. We patronize their president's bar out of respect, but at the end of the day we don't try to be them—because we aren't them.

The inside info that this retired officer provides is revealing and revolting. His words about the investigators who were both enamored of the biker lifestyle but also using it to muscle-up their own positions are especially cutting. It's kind of like the Bad-Bwana big-game hunter who respects and fears that king cat but has no problem using a .600 Overkill at long range to take it down and prove something.

Mano a mano is way, way too risky.

REACTION AND RESPONSE

Both the cops and the clubs have their sympathizers—and detractors—
so it's hard to keep all the "sensitive" info in-house forever.

There's an old biker saying: "Three can keep a secret if two are dead." In this case,
it's not quite to that level, but these cop-seminar secrets were spilled by a retired
Harley-riding officer who just got tired of shaking his head at all the bullshit.

PART V

Choppers, Classics, and Crusades

CHAPTER 20:

FLOATING ALONE

THE NIGHT TRAIN THAT TOOK TO THE OCEAN

INTERROGATING THE SUBJECT

Now we need to know a little something about these machines. Was that Harley that drifted from Japan to Canada just a curiosity or was it symbolic of something more?

It's been a little more than three years since the biggest earthquake in Japan's history, a quake that caused an unforgettable tsunami that killed some 20,000 people. But the earthquake also had quieter consequences that didn't make headlines. . . . People reported neighbors—neighbors who died in the tsunami—appearing at their houses and coming and sitting down in puddles of water.

—National Public Radio, March 16, 2014

S ix minutes is a long damn time to rock and roll in a 9.0 earthquake. Stuff like that can easily shock you into spirit sightings.

It was midafternoon on Friday, March 11, 2011, when the Tōhoku region of Japan, north of Tokyo, was hit with the country's worst earthquake and the fourth most powerful in modern recorded history.

Then the quake's tsunami rolled in.

Waves reached heights of one hundred thirty-three feet in Miyako, in Tōhoku's Iwate Prefecture. In the area of the city of Sendai, the ocean plowed six miles inland.

Honshu, the main island of Japan, was moved eight feet east, and the Earth's axis was shifted by between four and ten inches.

The "Great East Japan Earthquake" and its whirled water caused 15,893 deaths; left 6,152 injured; 2,572 missing; 127,290 buildings leveled; 272,788 "half leveled"; and another 747,989 "partially" leveled. The quake started fires, destroyed roads, twisted train tracks, and collapsed a dam.

It was a giant mother-faulter.

"WHO YOU GONNA CALL?"

Media coverage was almost as big as the swells and the shakes. In March 2014, National Public Radio (NPR) siphoned through one of the two strangest stories to ebb and flow in the aftermath years of the tsunami as they interviewed writer Richard Lloyd Parry.

Parry had documented the experiences of a Buddhist priest, Reverend Taio Kaneda, which added a lot of creepiness to the crawling social impact of the wild wave.

For starters, it seems that soon after the tsunami, people were coming to this priest with bodies they wanted him to bury. Then they told him stories of hauntings and supernatural events involving ghosts of people who had died in the tsunami. Other people saw spooky figures on the beach and there was one man who hated to go out because he saw eyes of people in puddles!

Then Reverend Kaneda encountered people who seemed possessed by the spirits of those who had died in the tragedy. Parry described one such possession of a man who had made a trip to the shore to see the effects of the tsunami:

He'd had no idea the devastation was so bad. But he came back that evening, sat down for dinner with his family, had his tea, a can of beer and then began rolling around on the ground making animal noises, running out into the field behind his house rolling in the mud, to the horror of his wife and his mother. He woke up the next day not knowing anything about this. And this continued for three days. He was talking in a strange guttural way, threatening violence, talking about the dead. His family were beside themselves and they eventually persuaded him to go to the priest who recited the Buddhist sutras and drove out these spirits, and he felt a lot better soon after that.

—Richard Lloyd Parry, National Public Radio, March 16, 2014

The mythical, mysterious, and salty ride of Ikuo Yokoyama's H is now enshrined at the Harley-Davidson Museum in Milwaukee. With every second of its slow disintegration, it powerfully builds itself up as the strongest memorial to victims of Japan's 2011 killer earthquake and tsunami. *Felicia Morgan*

Well, thank Buddha! Now we *all* feel a lot better.

But there was an even stranger story.

Sort of.

That is, if you believe in motorcycles more than you believe in ghosts.

ANOTHER MUDDY GHOST

In April 2012, as Canadian Peter Mark rode his ATV along the beach on Graham Island in British Columbia's Haida Gwaii Islands, he saw a large white cube. "Like the back part of a moving truck," he said, "just below the high-tide mark. The door was ripped off it and I could see a motorcycle tire sticking out, so I went closer and looked inside and saw a Harley-Davidson motorcycle."

Mark checked things out.

A Japanese license tag was still attached to the busted-up bike.

Another ghost was "rolling in the mud."

With the help of friends, two local Harley dealers—Steve Drane H-D and Deeley H-D—and the Japanese consulate in Vancouver, Peter Mark kicked the process into gear that would elevate the bike from curious rusted debris to being put on a pedestal for the symbol of survival that it is.

The bike was hauled into Victoria while the consulate traced the Harley's plates. It was registered to a person in Miyagi Prefecture, one of the most devastated of the tsunami areas. Was the owner even alive?

BRUISED AND BATTERED BUT NOT BEATEN

Facts were surfacing.

The bike was a 2004 Night Train, belonging to a twenty-nine-year-old man named Ikuo Yokoyama. He had used the container as a storage shed for the bike, camping equipment, and golf clubs. The tsunami sucked all those toys out to sea in a hurry when it roared over Ikuo's town.

A year and a four-thousand-mile bumpy cruise later, what was left of those toys had been scattered on a Canadian beach.

The first thoughts from the benevolent H-D guys were to restore the bike and give it back to its owner—but that changed. As upwards of a thousand people showed up to look at the bike at Steve Drane's British Columbia dealership, Drane noticed something.

"I watched people looking at it," he told the press. "The expressions on their faces told me 'You've got to leave it the way it is.'"

The Harley-Davidson Museum in Milwaukee—the bike's now agreed-upon ultimate destination—concurred. More importantly, so did Ikuo.

The Power of Nature

Metals like steel and aluminum, along with rubber, plastics and leather, all deteriorate. Add in moisture, oxygen, and salt, and the process intensifies, particularly for metal. While the trailer holding this motorcycle was adrift, some seawater was likely inside, causing initial corrosion. The destruction rapidly increased after the motorcycle was washed out of the trailer and onto the beach. Laying on its left side, the bike was pounded with water and dragged over the sand and rocks by the tide. The resulting mechanical damage breached the bike's surface finishes like paint and chrome plating, leaving parts vulnerable to the salt water. The surfaces on other parts, such as the chromed oil lines on the right side, were not broken. Therefore they do not show much corrosion at all.

The Harley-Davidson Museum's description for Ikuo Yokoyama's bike.
Felicia Morgan

He asked that Harley place the bike in the museum—in its battered state—as a memorial to victims of the earthquake and tsunami. Ikuo didn't just lose his Harley; he also lost his home and three family members.

This was now about the preservation of solid memories, not flitting ghosts.

RUST, RESPECT, AND REVERENCE

But in Milwaukee, a kind of an exorcism would be performed. The museum's metal magicians had to figure out the best way to keep the skeleton alive. The Night Train was decomposing.

"Some of the chrome still looked good and the tires were in okay shape," Kristen Jones, senior curator at the museum, explained to the press. "The rest of the bike, not so much. . . . If we washed the sand and salt off, we would be taking something away from the story. . . .

"It was really important that we treat the bike with respect and reverence. It was part of someone's life that was torn apart."

The bike will continue to deteriorate, but as with the *Mona Lisa* at the Louvre, the Milwaukee masterminds have a controlled climate and environment to give the bike as long a life as possible.

Eventually, Ikuo will make the journey—more comfortably than his bike, it's hoped—to North America to meet Peter Mark and to visit the museum. But for now, several years later, he is still "busy rebuilding his life."

And from the human-most perspective, the museum display is helping with that. To look at that bike is haunting.

It's the perfect symbol.

It's a symbol of tough survival.

And the universal love and respect for a big bike is the best totem of all to tie the world emotionally together. Some things need no translation.

REACTION AND RESPONSE

Ikuo Yokoyama's Night Train proved, once again, just what a global icon the American V-twin is. The respect and reverence given to the bike and what it represents elevates the human spirit, even when hit with one of the most high-profile natural disasters the planet has seen in modern times.

CHAPTER 21:

"GIMME A BIKE ON THE ROCKS, PLEASE…"

THE FIFTY-SIX-YEAR FREEZE OF A 1938 GERMAN NSU

INTERROGATING THE SUBJECT
You can't be serious: machines really have a "soul"?

> When machine guns were carried on mules in the old way, from two to
> four minutes were required to set up and begin firing. The motorcycle
> machine gun permits of instant firing from the sidecar....
> —The *Enthusiast*, 1916

Military bikes are some of the coolest examples of "the soul in the machine."
They're like Charlie Daniels's "Talk to Me Fiddle" song: a wish that you could
look into the long life of some well-worn instrument—or motorcycle—that has
been in hand after hand and had experience after experience around the world.

Tell us about the battles you were in, the battering you took, the bullets you
dodged, the drunks that let you fall, the passion or desperation in the way you
were ridden.

"IT'S ALIVE! IT'S ALIVE!"

In 1873, a knitting-machine manufacturer, Mechanische Werkstätte zur Herstellung
von Strickmaschinen, was established in the town of Riedlingen on the Danube. Man,
that alone sounds like the makings of a song Charlie's fiddle might have played before it
"came across the sea"—when it was still called a violin. *Now, for your listening pleasure,
"Riedlingen on the Danube in E-minor" by Herr Gewürztraminer....*

By 1892, knitting-machine production gave way to bicycle-building, and the
company's long, long German name became NSU (Neckarsulm Strickmaschinen
Union). Then came the bikes with engines. NSU produced its first motorcycle in 1901,
the same year that Indian fired up in America and two years before Harley-Davidson. In
1905, they added cars to their assembly lines.

By World War II, NSU was not only supplying motorcycles to the German military
but creating other vehicles, too—vehicles that looked like Frankenstein-fabricated fit-
togethers of bikes, half-tracks, cars, and tanks. Talk about myths, mysteries, and rumors;
their *Kettenkrad* creature, in particular, looked like what you might get if a Panzer tank
rear-ended an Amazonas.

But their good ol' normal motorcycles came in six models, including a V-Twin.
Down through the years, NSU bikes were racetrack terrors, setting record after record.

The 251 OSL model used in World War II was a 242cc, single-cylinder four-stroke.
It was a pretty cool bike for a soldier to "rescue" from the war.

And that's exactly what a veteran-soon-to-turn-farmer would do.

A BIG SWAN DIVE

The vet returned home from World War II Germany—with the NSU—and settled near Dassel, Minnesota. Dassel, known for its Red Rooster Days over Labor Day Weekend, takes up a very small spot in the south-central part of the state. And being in the "Land of 10,000 Lakes," Dassel is yes, near a lake; several lakes, actually, including Big Swan Lake about five miles outside of town.

How much that vet-turned-man-of-the-soil ever used that NSU is unknown, but what *is* known is that in 1956 another of Dassel's folks, a guy named Wyman Ailie, bought the motorcycle for his then-fifteen-year-old son, Dean.

December in Minnesota usually means a hard-freeze for those lakes, but Big Swan apparently had a big crack. Dean Ailie went for a ride with some friends, but his homeward shortcut across the lake didn't go well. Bike and rider broke through the ice; myths and rumors have Dean being buoyed by air trapped in his leather jacket, keeping him up long enough to be saved by some fishermen.

The NSU unfortunately had nothing like that in the way of impromptu water wings, so the motorcycle became a quick anchor.

RIP, NSU.

After fifty-six years, the soul-filled NSU's chilly rest was over. Since its warm reunion with owner Dean Ailie, the worldly war ride has enjoyed honors like this cool display in a big Nebraska bike show. *Felicia Morgan*

"HE'S JUST RESTING, WAITING FOR A NEW LIFE TO COME"

The NSU-Frankenstein connection may have had something to do with what happened many, many years later. There in the winter dampness of Minnesota's Meeker County, on November 29, 2012, fisherman Ken Seemann's nets were set for carp, but they snagged a 'cycle. After fifty-six years, the NSU's chilly rest was over.

Dassel was a small town in '56 and the news of teen Dean's dive had traveled fast. In 2012, the good news of the recovery operation traveled even faster. Dassel's then-population of about fifteen hundred included some folks who still remembered The Big Crack of 1956. It was no mystery as to whose bike it was. At seventy-one years of age, Dean—still a local—was reunited with his NSU.

So, what kind of shape is the German scooter in? Motorcycle.com reported that "considering how long it sat at the bottom of the lake, the motorcycle is in a surprisingly good condition. It was coated in rust, the seat had long dissolved and the fuel tank has some holes, but the cylinder was dry and the tires still contained some air."

As for the future, "Ailie...was in tears when the bike was brought to him. Ailie told local reporters that the bike will be given to a local restorer, Ron Miller, who has agreed to restore the bike as best as can be done (it will never run again), and display it with a placard telling the story of its drowning, and recovery. Ailie told Miller all he wants is a photo of the bike once it's restored," according to USRiderNews.com.

Well, the news did a fine job of wrapping up the facts about the bike's underwater show 'n' shine aesthetics and the what-nexts. But the intangibles in something like this are what really count. The intangibles are what infuse the imagination. This machine has such a soul and such a story—from a World War II rescue to kicking up fertile dust in a Minnesota farmland to fifty-six years at the bottom of an often-frozen lake.

Damn it—talk to me, motorcycle!

REACTION AND RESPONSE

Machines absolutely have souls; especially when it comes to motorcycles. Especially when it comes to *old* motorcycles. Add in some things like a world war, rolling on two continents, and a half-century entombment to their lifespan, and you have a holy spirit with even more power and even more passion. Ask anyone who has ever loved, owned, sold, lost, or wanted back a 1938 *anything*.

CHAPTER 22:

EXHUMING AL'S BABY

BACK-ENGINEERING THE CROCKER MOTORCYCLE

INTERROGATING THE SUBJECT

Was the Crocker the best V-twin ever produced? Better than Indian? Better than Harley? And is it really experiencing the miracle of a second coming?

When the first Crocker road machines blasted onto the scene in 1936, it astonished the motorcycling community and "single-handedly caused Harley-Davidson and Indian more grief than any event up to the British motorcycle invasion of the 1950s."

—*Iron Horse*, April 1979

Meet Al.

Al Crocker was born a while back, in 1882.

He was a good guy and an interesting dude.

He earned an engineering degree, a tough challenge at the turn of *that* century. He found his first employment at Thor Motorcycle, where he engineered new products. He loved motorcycle-riding and racing, and that led him to a friendship with Oscar Hedstrom and Charles Hendee of Indian Motorcycles, and a full-time position at their company.

That got him the Indian dealership in Kansas City, Missouri. From there, Al moved to the West Coast, where he bought another Indian shop.

Cool.

But this is where the simple business-wise story of Albert Crocker becomes heavyweight motorcycling history; with myths and mysteries of a bike that out-legends both Indian and Harley.

Back-engineering every detail of Al Crocker's masterpiece has allowed visionary Michael Schacht to perform the miracle of Crocker's continued production, not merely a modern reproduction. *Courtesy Michael Schacht and the Crocker Motorcycle Co.*

169

NO REFUNDS!

Settled in Los Angeles, Al and his shop foreman, Paul Bigsby, began designing and developing their own bikes. In 1931 they introduced their dirt-track racers, and then later, the Crocker 30–50 cubic-inch single-cylinder speedway bike. Al and Paul's machines were kicking oval-course ass.

By the mid-1930s, Crocker and Bigsby were dreaming—and building—bigger. From 1936 to 1942, about three hundred full-size, high-performance, overhead-valve V-twins were produced, with approximately eighty surviving today.

The production number is a controversial one in itself, one more mystery that muddles the Crocker myths. But the truth is that Al Crocker was an exacting man and his numbering system did indeed reach into the three-hundred range. Factor in the power of the bikes, and a fair amount of them *must* have come to a high-speed end!

Referred to as "Big Tank" and "Small Tank" models, they looked good and ran like hungry jackals in a petting zoo, with cruising speeds of about 120-plus mph right out of the box.

And the Crocker customer was also a big part of the "Commitment to Excellence" of *this* Al. Each bike was custom-tailored to the individual rider's order—color, the amount of chrome trim, and even displacement. Then came the guarantee that the full purchase price would be refunded if the buyer was beaten by a factory stock Harley or Indian!

That never happened.

A HIGH-SPEED END

But then the bombs of World War II hit.

Indian and Harley got fat Army contracts; Al got his with Douglas Aircraft, making plane parts. It was better and bigger business than the bikes, and so, by 1942, Crocker motorcycles had taken their last production ride. Crocker Motorcycle became Crocker Manufacturing, and all of *that* was eventually sold to a little ol' auto-super-product company called BorgWarner.

And for those of you who have ever picked up and picked *on* a high-end axe, you may have experienced what Paul Bigsby went on to do in the way of guitars, tailpieces, and tremolos.

Both Al and Paul sure left their mega-marks on more than one part of American society and industry. But man, those bikes...

Today, the surviving Crockers are more than just relics: they are geared gods to be worshipped by those who understand and appreciate the engineering in these machines.

And they ain't cheap.

Vintage Crockers have fiery flirtations with the $400K range and go up from there according to their purity of pedigree.

"We've been focused on the metallurgy and on the quality of those castings," says Crocker's Michael Schacht. "And of course our parts retrofit original Crockers. We've been selling our OEM parts for years." *Bill Hayes, courtesy Michael Schacht and the Crocker Motorcycle Co.*

AN ADVENTURE AND A DREAM

After extensively studying the mind and machine of Albert Crocker, visionary and vintage bike superhero Michael Schacht set out to honor both with a new life. In 1992 Michael began to revive the Crocker Motorcycle Company. But he didn't just buy the name and slap it on a modern machine. Using the *exact* specifications developed by Al in his Los Angeles factory in the 1930s, Michael's savior of a company began producing authentic Crocker parts—and complete bikes. In early 2008, the operation was fittingly moved back to its Los Angeles origin, where the Second Coming could be continued on especially holy ground.

Michael Schacht relives the ride:

> This whole thing for me has not only been an adventure and a dream, but it has also been a permanent learning curve. I was very naïve and excited going into this. I wanted to recreate what Al Crocker built—with all the beauty and all the nuances. Ironically, with perfect re-creation, we engineered it all, including all the original inherent problems that were in that beautiful machine. Faults happened because it was so exact to the original.
>
> I've spent the last few years in R&D; slowly, one step at a time changing all of that. We are very close now to perfection. We're just putting the final strokes on the clutch and the gearbox—a bit of a challenge because we have manufactured everything in both. We're dealing with the stack and the shimming and putting some thrust bearings in that didn't exist before. We even make our own clutch plates. All the changes were internal; nothing external or visible. The bike is a one hundred percent fit-the-box identical version.
>
> We even engineered the leaking cases out of the equation. The new Crockers will no longer leak—although the prototype does! And in the prototype that's a tough fix unless we change the engine cases so we're going to leave that one alone! Hey, all vintage bikes like to mark their spot! But the new Crockers beyond the prototype won't leak!
>
> Also, we've been focused on the metallurgy and on the castings and the quality of those castings. And of course our parts retrofit original Crockers. We've been selling our OEM parts for years.
>
> Bringing the company back to Los Angeles, where it all began, allowed me to access some of the industry's finest engineers—with the exacting skill and quality of Southern California's aerospace legacy. Our team that includes my right-hand man and chief

engineer, Patrick Folger, and pattern makers, Olie Kiprianoff and Brian McCabe is precision personified.

This motorcycle is not a reproduction but a continued production of Al Crocker's masterpiece.

NAY-SAYERS AND NOBLE DREAMERS

But miracle workers always have their skeptics. Michael was not immune:

> Many said it could never be done, especially to this exacting of a degree. But I begged to differ! We have a lot of proof now. Some of the greatest Crocker aficionados on the planet all agree that what we have produced is an incredible bike.
>
> One of our biggest supporters was the late Chuck Vernon, who passed away recently, well into his nineties. Chuck was one of the true keepers of the Crocker grail after Ernie Skelton. It was an honor to know him, be friends with him, to have a pat on the back from him. He was always supportive of us against the nay-sayers—and yes, we had our share of negativity.

The Crocker story has myths and mysteries that "out-legend" both Indian and Harley. *Bill Hayes, courtesy Michael Schacht and the Crocker Motorcycle Co.*

There's a legitimate comparison to the Tucker automobile saga here. At first, people were very excited when they heard the story. Then we heard things like, "Can you believe what these 'dreamers' are trying to do? It'll never work...but it's noble!"

To a lot of people we were just that: "dreamers."

But when I started to produce the products, man did things change! We wound up with plenty of those nay-sayers buying parts from us.

BIG UNVEIL AT THE QUAIL

The newly reborn Crocker didn't just outrun the doubters; it won over the industry.

In 2012, we had just finished some final testing on our Big Tank prototype bike and it was ready to unveil. At about that same time The Quail Motorsports Gathering in Carmel, California, contacted us to bring the Crocker up there. The Quail event is the most prestigious motorcycle event in the world; huge and universally well-respected. They were very excited to have us there.

Our Crocker was an instant hit. We were just swamped by people the whole time we were there. When we fired the bike up, not only were there cameras all around but they also placed a PA mic right near the engine; the entire facility heard the roar!

When I came back to our display tent after lunch I had a little tag on the bike and the crowd was jumping up and down: "You won something! You won something!"

I thought maybe I'd won a t-shirt or something but Paul d'Orléans from The Vintagegent vintage bike site was telling me to get the bike up on the podium! "In about two minutes you're going to be honored with the Quail Industry Award."

It's a truly great and prestigious honor.

This type of industry recognition is a wonderful part of that "proof."

A LITTLE AND A LOT

"We've seen a lot of original Crockers over the years," Michael recalls, thinking back on all he has witnessed in the bike's evolution and resurrection, "and many of them had crude, hand-made replacement parts. Obviously, they can't compare to our bike."

> What we have done is really in the vein of Al Crocker. We think he would have been very proud of this project and very excited to see how we worked with his beautiful product.
>
> We didn't change it a bit, but changed it a lot, all at the same time.
>
> Even in modern times, this bike is amazing to ride. I was asked to be the ambassador in the Distinguished Gentleman's Ride last year aboard our Crocker. I rode out front and stayed out front. In a sea of hundreds of bikes—some good riders, some bad riders, some non-riders—it performed like the champ it is; in spite of foot clutch, hand shift, and manual spark advance!
>
> We are very proud of this machine.
>
> It's a testimony to Al Crocker's incredible design.
>
> And ultimately, it's a tribute to Al Crocker, the man.

It's also a tribute to Michael Schacht. To his determination, to his unbelievable monetary and personal sacrifices, and to a life of dedication to give new life to what is considered by many to have been the best V-twin ever produced.

REACTION AND RESPONSE

When a seventy-plus-year-old motorcycle can sell for $400,000 on up to a million, it's a pretty good indication that it—and its marque—are special. Maybe the *most* special. And the back-engineering of Crocker motorcycles, to keep them exactly as they were, is absolutely a miracle! Especially in this "tears of a clone" era of facsimiles and fakes.

CHAPTER 23:

EXTREME AND INSANE

THE MYSTERIES OF THE MOST GRUELING SOLO TRIPS EVER ATTEMPTED: WHO TAKES THEM... AND WHY

INTERROGATING THE SUBJECT

What compels these riders to do their *Mission Impossible* stunts? Is it just for thrills, or is it something deeper?

> The Pan, my only partner for many miles, was a fun contraption with a foot clutch and hand shifter.... Rides took on a life of their own; a relationship [developed] between me and the bike as highways, features, and elements became animated. Einstein was right. Space and time do warp; after a day's ride, distance and hours felt like a blip.
>
> —Mike Rinowski, *Harley Tracks: Across Vietnam to The Wall*

S olo rides are therapeutic.
We all take them.
Those are the special, gotta-clear-the-head times when you don't call anyone to come along and you don't head for the places where you know friends will be. It's just you, the bike, and that old Chuck Berry no-particular-place-to-go attitude.

But therapy, like everything else, has its degrees of intensity. There's a wide gap between clearing your head and conquering the world—but the motorcycle is, of course, the perfect tool for both.

BARTERING TEQUILA FOR GAS

Most of us aren't part of that second bunch. World-conquering requires an icy DNA that's not wired into every swingin' data mine; but a few have it. A few have savored it and cultivated it and—together with a bike—have conquered not only some of the toughest parts of this planet but some of the toughest parts of the human psyche as well. Fears, physical frailties, quests, bucket lists, and just-because-it's-there restlessness have all been the starting lines for "impossible" rides.

It's not a new therapy, either. In the early 1950s, L.A. motorcycling legend Les Haserot became known as the "Baja King" because of his many solo trips from Southern California to La Paz, Mexico—over a thousand miles of bad roads, trails, washes, deep sand, mud, trading tequila with farmers for gummed-up gas, and offended *policía* who objected to Les's 1937 45 being painted like the Mexican flag. But he loved every second of it, still telling the stories of his long-life-giving "therapy" until he passed away in his eighties; and still spirit-strong with that icy DNA.

But since the days of the Baja King, the DNA has gotten even icier and steelier; the rides have gotten longer; and your basic dangers have been replaced by 360-degree global peril.

The good news is that it seems the therapy end of this has heated up right in ratio to the frigidity of the nerves.

"LIFE IS GREAT!"

The Iron Butt Association—"World's Toughest Riders"—has more than fifty thousand members. Extreme and insane rides are a big part of what they do. They chronicle the rides, certify the rides, and write about the rides.

So much of their mindset appears to slide into that because-it's-there slot. Pure, unbending, and determined endurance is their fuel of choice.

One of their most prominent members was the late Ron "Moto Guzzi Ron" Ayres. Successful in a corporate career, Ron went on to develop Ayres Adventures, a global motorcycle travel company that took two-wheelers all over the world. He also authored three books, one of which was *Against the Clock*, about his quickie-pleasure putt through forty-nine states in seven days.

According to those close to him, Ron was still riding "nonstop" into his seventies, and reminiscent of Les Haserot, "Life is great" was his ageless motorcycling mantra.

Ron's solo-shot up to the North Pole is more than legendary and more than epic. What he experienced, suffered, and survived skyrocketed the term "iron butt" to iron *will*. That trip wasn't about miles and hours; it was about animals, roads that aren't really roads, total desolation, and learning local law.

And it's in those kinds of extremes where the real inner-gut exploration of these lone-sharks begins.

THE ICE MAN LIST

Think about all the times you've heard modern urban riders complain, bellyache, or creak in their bones after a "blistering" five-hour ride, or maybe even after finally slapping down that elusive monumental pilgrimage to Sturgis.

Then look at the real Ice Man list.

Les "Baja King" Haserot's Mexican-flag-motif '37 got him into a little *agua caliente* with south-of-the-border authorities during his long early solo trips from SoCal into La Paz. *Bill Hayes*

Besides Haserot and Ayres, you have to add guys such as the Bay Area's Miles Davis —no, not the jazz giant; *this* Miles's horn is on his bike—who spent years on his Royal Enfield in the crowded heat of India. On one hand, his remote riding is ecstasy:

> It occurs to me that except for a few ridiculous conversations about Indian food, I have hardly spoken all day. It has been a journey of meditative bliss on two wheels, a good day and a great ride. So good, in fact, that if I am called from this world here and now, I would leave entirely fulfilled and satisfied.
> —Miles Davis, *Motorcycle Yoga: Meditative Rides through India*

On the other hand, there's always that strong appetite for survival that transcends transcendentalism:

> Breaking free from the mob of megaliths, I gun the bike through the three upper gears until the speedo shows 65 kmh upon a stretch of paved roadway. I must put some space between the bike and any of the trucks that are lumbering after me. When roads narrow to the width of one lane, the Tatas [Indian diesel trucks] can be impossible to get around and precious life in this land of one billion quickly becomes cheap. Cheap, that is, in the estimation of others. Even an insect, like an ant or a fly, will try to save itself and I'm no different.... No one wants to die unsung and alone in this third world. Indeed, death has but few volunteers.

Somehow, desperate, deserted, and dangerous feelings like this are seldom experienced on roads like I-90 between Sundance and Sturgis. Even in the middle of the night in a South Dakota summer storm, life is never "cheap"—and besides, Spearfish is just ahead.

SPIRITS OVER THE 17TH PARALLEL

Mike Rinowski is another for the list. His ride—and rides—across Vietnam in memory of our war vets help us to never forget:

> The National Highway lay empty below a low, gray sky. A damp chill attacked through the gaps around my jacket, but my facemask added a new warmth. From Dong Ha, I roared toward Khe Sanh, but dismal weather soon slowed me to a crawl. I hadn't hit elevations yet, and I knew it would only get worse. I considered a two-day ride

over the Western Branch, but with less than a blanket or a tent, that was not a good idea. I decided I would carry the spirits over it on my return, and I backtracked to the Eastern Branch for a crossover near the 17th parallel, where construction pushed me into another retreat.

I held steady over a bleak landscape . . . nine hours and 250 miles from Hue. . . .

—*Harley Tracks*

From the roads of Vietnam, Mike traveled to the comparative ease of American interstates as he "fulfilled" his memorial journey by making the Run to The Wall. Again, everything is measured by degree:

Across the Iowa state line, I looked to a group of wind generators I remembered from ten years earlier, and then recalled a family that once lived near generators in Vietnam. I wanted to believe the father worked at the new power plant near them and afforded education for his sons. Today, a thousand gigantic blades sliced through spacious skies above me. I crept past a seventies Pontiac ragtop, and the young at heart waved from their breezy seats. While I powered south, a sight on my horizon held a familiar shade of dark, and then a reckless band of white and gold flashed across it as a warning or a dare. I laughed about my ride off the mountain [in Vietnam] and exited when the first sprinkles hit the windshield.

Hell yes! Get in out of the rain, Mike. You've earned it.

The iron butts—and iron wills—of Les, Ron, Miles, and Mike have made them super-worthy of their places on the "list," but now we get into a different species of Ice Man altogether. Three guys especially have conquered the world and conquered themselves on a bike. Remember them when you're hot, cold, hungry, struggling with what music to program into your iPhone, or sweating the next gas stop while on reserve—things can always be worse. At least you're not being tortured by Colombian drug lords, riding 83,000 miles with two prosthetic legs, or all alone on a bike in the most remote corner of this planet.

TWO WHEELS THROUGH TERROR

Glen Heggstad is part of that goal-achievement—and restless—wing of the extreme-and-insane ride bunch. A Palm Springs martial arts teacher, he was getting itchy:

After retiring from martial arts competition in 1999, I moved out to the country to seek inner peace as a mild-mannered judo instructor.

Life was decelerating at a pace that I feared was grinding to a halt. I still kept a motorcycle for primary transportation and lightweight thrills but seldom ventured out of California anymore. I craved one last hoorah, a journey somewhere into the unpredictable to wake me up.

—Glen Heggstad, *Two Wheels Through Terror*

The journey "somewhere" ended up being a run from the swank SoCal desert to the bottom tip of South America.

And back.

Alone.

That'll sure as hell "wake you up."

Or kill you.

Almost from the beginning, the latter was a distinct probability for Heggstad:

There's no place to pull over, no gas stations or restaurants, and the only lights are the dreaded approaching painful high beams that send me reeling into vertigo.

Life is a statistical risk and the odds of making it to safety tonight are heavily out of favor. Even the years of training, the research, and high-tech equipment couldn't prepare me for this. All that's left is to play the cards viciously flung at me as a question echoes in the back of my mind: "Would I trade places with any other man on Earth?" The answer is still a resounding, "No."

The sheer *tamaño y magnitud* of Glen's odyssey is much too far out for mortal humans to grasp. With all that he has to deal with in the way of mechanical problems, weather, thieves, and the region's volatile political climate, this experience is on a plane much closer to sick fantasy than comprehendible fact.

As we've seen, however, things can always be worse. When Glen hit Colombia, everything really went south:

Slowly emerging from the haze of my fading dream—dismally recalling events leading to this stomach-burning moment, I return to the savage nightmare of reality. It's true. I'm here in the mountains of Colombia, a prisoner of a violent Marxist terrorist army, deep in a chilly wilderness far from the people I love, people who don't yet know that I am missing. Images of a happy life in California flicker into the back of my mind as I now must focus on a moment-to-moment struggle to stay alive. The motorcycle adventure of a lifetime has become two wheels through terror. I sit trying to remember how this all started out.

It wasn't easy, but a hunger strike and some other wrangling finally gains Heggstad his freedom after weeks in captivity. He is turned over to Red Cross and FBI officials:

> "Yes, we have arranged a flight home for you."
>
> "Thanks guys, but that's not where I want to go"...With a crazed look in my eye I state, "I am going back after my fucking motorcycle and finishing my fucking ride to fucking Argentina."
>
> "That's impossible. You have no documents, passport, or money."
>
> "I will have money wired and get a new passport issued at the Embassy...."
>
> The best way to give the middle finger to the ELN [the terrorist kidnappers] and show the world that terrorism against Americans doesn't work is to finish my ride after they tried so hard to break my spirit and destroy my soul....I cannot give in and return home. It will destroy me as a man.

In May of 2002, Glen's "last hoorah" wake-up call came full circle as he—and his icy will—rolled into the springtime heat of Palm Springs after six months on the road.

He was right—completing that ride was the ideal way to tell those terrorists to go *tornillo* themselves.

LYING DOWN WITH THE LIONS

On August 29, 1981, Vietnam vet and then-member of the South African Defence Force Dave Barr was in a non-armored vehicle that hit a land mine in Angola. The result was the loss of both his legs.

Nine years later, Barr would climb on a '72 Shovel and ride around the world, covering six continents and over 83,000 miles in three and a half years. Barr's trip upped the ante in its extreme and insane gamble due to its mass of miles, the extended time he spent, and his trying to survive in desolate places. Plus that other factor of having no legs!

This cutting combination can take a rider to a very sheer edge—like Barr's tough day in the Namib desert:

> On my first day on a dirt road, I got a little bit cocky, going too far in one day...about 300 miles, averaging too fast a speed—about 50 miles per hour. When my tires dug into some deep gravel, the

Harley wobbled and threw me off. I landed on my knees, then my elbows, then the motorcycle landed on me! It felt like a freight train as it came from behind and knocked me flat into the gravel and sand! Then, it went flipping along on its own, coming to rest on its kickstand, sitting on its wheels!

Never let it be said that the Harley-Davidson Motor Company "don't make good kickstands!"

Flat on the ground in pain, the first thing I did was search for my heavy caliber revolver. There are lions in the Namib Desert, and there are the roaming Namas, a desert people who can also be hazardous to one's health.

When I located the revolver, I cleaned it out the best I could. It was hard to move! Incredible pain punished my pelvis and ribs. Later, I would learn that my pelvis and two ribs were cracked.

—Dave Barr, *Riding the Edge*

Dave Barr's 'round-the-world whirl was also unique in purpose, ramping up from personal goals to setting an example to the physically challenged of the world, showing them what they are capable of. Global media coverage helped further the message.

Dave's Shovel is on display at the AMA Motorcycle Hall of Fame in Pickerington, Ohio, and he was inducted into the Motorcycle Hall of Fame in 2000.

"EMPTINESS CAN BE BEAUTIFUL, AND INTENSELY TERRIFYING"

One ride that may be the absolute bedrock ultimate in man-versus-machine-versus-nature had no global media—or any outside media at all—to cover it. The rider himself was the media.

And he may be the coolest of the big league Ice Men.

India native Gaurav Jani combined a goal, a just-because-it's-there, and ultra-endurance, when he saddled up alone and headed out from Mumbai (formerly Bombay) to reach one of the most remote places in the world, the Changthang Plateau in Ladakh, on the border of China.

Look it up on a world map.

It'll make you shiver and slap your forehead.

Imagine the most desolate places you've ridden through; then laugh at them. They're about as barren as the food court at your local mall at Christmas when compared to the Changthang Plateau.

About the region, travel writer Bibek Bhattacharya has said, "Emptiness can be beautiful, and intensely terrifying. . . . the Changthang is a profoundly eerie and wonderful place."

Cool, but "emptiness" and "eerie" also mean that the area lacks a few things: things such as roads, motels, restaurants, gas stations, civilization, and the oxygen that is much more plentiful at elevations below fifteen thousand feet.

THE DARK SIDE OF THE MOON MEETS THE GARDEN OF EDEN

The goal portion of Gaurav's trip was to have an "adventure ride" and to film everything. The result was indeed an adventure and an award-winning documentary called *Riding Solo to the Top of the World*.

The bike that Gaurav used was his personal ride, a five-year-old Royal Enfield (no surprise here, Enfields are still manufactured in India). "I didn't have a lineup of bikes from which I could choose," says Gaurav, so his own bike was pretty much the only option.

It was loaded up, bungied, and strapped with camera gear, gas, and supplies for the seventy-day trip, resembling something between a Conestoga wagon headed for the Gold Rush and the fleets of shopping-cart commandos sipping bum-wine behind a dumpster down in the Tenderloin.

Leaving the mobbed urban scene of India's cities, Gaurav indicates that he will stay off the main thoroughfares and take only the "back roads"—and "back roads" in India redefine the term. They are *way* back, and for the most part, they aren't exactly "roads."

Gaurav rides—and sometimes pushes—that bike through, over, and around areas that get crazier and crazier in terms of that "intensely terrifying emptiness."

Once he reaches the areas of northeast India, here come those altitudes, ranging from 15,000 to 18,634 feet at the site of the highest road in the world at Marsimik La. At heights like that, you—and your bike—may as well be trying to breathe on Pluto. The lack of air takes its toll on both Gaurav and the Enfield, but the desolation is so sharply hypnotic in its beauty that its siren-like allure seems to counterbalance the physical torture. It's the dark side of the moon in its vastness and its bleakness; it's the Garden of Eden in lushness and seduction.

THE REAL TAKEAWAY IN EXTREME AND INSANE

As if the ride itself isn't enough, Gaurav's filming of it is difficult and tedious. To get riding shots and long-range panoramas of himself, he'd set up his camera, ride his bike out yonder, then have to come back for his equipment—often running up and down mountains, having left his stuff's safety "up to the gods."

That "safety" factor brings up a compelling subplot of this trip: Gaurav's lack of bullet-dodging prowess and his non-concern for always-impending arrest and imprisonment that other epic solo riders have had to contend with. While Gaurav is warned about the "disputed territory" and to not cross over the border into China, he is essentially free of military-political intimidation. At least in this respect, Gaurav could more or less ride easy.

This tortuous trek and the film documentary as well—like every other part of this lifestyle—aren't just about motorcycles or a motorcycle trip. The adventure is ultimately about people: the person riding that bike and the people he meets. But in this case, in this environment, both are again far beyond what most Westerners are used to. This isn't "Spider" and "Six-Pack" heading out on new twin-cams, getting ready to whoop it up in Daytona.

No.

When Gaurav arrives at his turnaround point of the Changthang Plateau ("Changthang" aptly translates as "the land of less people"), he spends quite a bit of quality time with the local nomads, the Changpas.

Here is the real story.

Here is where Gaurav's "adventure trip" takes a turn.

Here are people who live a life of the fiercest kind of independence—with the kind of strength most of us would like to have in our emotional résumé (albeit in a bit more hospitable, indoor-plumbing and electricity-equipped society).

Gaurav establishes a serious bond and respect in his time with the nomads, especially with their leader, a man he describes as being "completely happy with himself and his surroundings, which is more than I could say for most of us." A man who lives under conditions that are sometimes so harsh they would have many of us squealing and crying like crushed crows—but a man who is truly one with his nature; a nature not encumbered by things such as modern societal constraints or four walls.

Maybe the main takeaway from Gaurav's Big Adventure is that it proves that no matter where you are in the world, whether you're on a motorcycle in the middle of total nowhere, in the swirl of a dense urban people-pool, or shepherding yaks along the slopes of the Tibetan Himalayas, that common human denominator is the desire to be free and unchained—a desire that some particularly strong individuals actually live out, regardless of the risk or struggle.

REACTION AND RESPONSE

These extreme riders all have personal driving forces, and their rides aren't "stunts." Thankfully, there are still get-off-the-couch warriors out there who will push themselves—and their machines—to near-lunatic limits to wring the most out of life.

CHAPTER 24:

CAPTAIN AMERICA'S AND BILLY'S WRECKED RIDES

WHAT REALLY HAPPENED TO THE *EASY RIDER* BIKES?

INTERROGATING THE SUBJECT

Will we ever truly know who built 'em, who stole 'em, and just what closet the skeletons are in now?

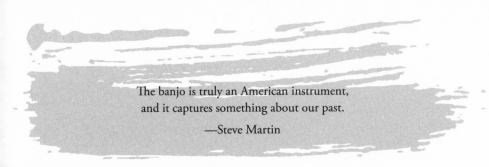

P robably two scenes in all of modern cinema haunt road-trippers when they find themselves rolling through the still-raw ends of remote 'n' rustic rural America. One is the sweaty "squeal like a pig" showstopper in *Deliverance*.

Soooooooey!

The other one comes at about the ninety-one-minute mark in 1969's generation-jolting *Easy Rider*. To the hammer chords of the Byrds' version of Dylan's "It's Alright, Ma (I'm Only Bleeding)," the flick begins to wind down. The road to "look for America" is now a fringe country two-lane, straight and eerily isolated.

Two tooth-challenged good ol' boys in a faded blue pickup truck roll up from behind and shotgun the film's existential heroes—and their bikes—into pieces.

"Why don't you get a haircut?" was the trigger man's question.

Why indeed?

Welcome to the end of the '60s.

"I CAN'T GET THOSE IMAGES OUT OF MY HEAD!"

Well, of the two disasters, we all know what happened to poor Ned Beatty (playing the character of Bobby Trippe). *Deliverance* was his debut motion picture and never again could he be looked at—either in person or on the silver screen—without an immediate vision of him being slopped with mud and having his not-so-tighty whities down around his ankles. It was an incredibly grinding—yet honorable—self-sacrifice for art.

But in the second messy climax, what the hell happened to those bikes?

The myths, mysteries, and rumors of the Panheads' premature demise really begin at their slightly breeched birth. They ironically backed into anti-establishment esteem as police mounts.

In those years of constant civil convulsion when *Easy Rider* was filmed, The Factory wasn't about to hand over some of their fresh new spiffy electric-start Shovelheads to hippies—even film-connected ones. According to a 2005 History Channel magazine article, the H-D gods weren't parting with any of their fine iron for the flick, because "The protagonists were outlaws and they thought it was bad for their image."

And so, most secret-sources agree, Fonda himself went to a police auction and bought four Hydra-Glide Pans for five hundred bucks. Two would be the main rides; two would be backups in case "anything went wrong." But seriously, what could possibly go wrong with a mix that included cop-worn chopped Panheads, drugs, the tilt-a-whirl '60s surroundings, angry armed rednecks, Peter Fonda, Jack Nicholson, and the ever-demure Dennis Hopper?

More mysteries, however, have sources arm-wrestling over the actual model years of the cop-classics, most with a reported span from 1949 to 1954. The ultra-detailed, scoop-specific movie info and trivia site IMDb.com says that all four were '62s, but then they *also* say that the bikes were a three-outta-four combination from '49, '50, and '52.

But the building of the bikes is where the most gummed-up of the birth stickiness starts.

"THE PARTICIPATION OF BLACKS…COMPLETELY SUPPRESSED"

There is little question that the police Pans were primarily transformed at the hands of now-legendary builders Ben Hardy and Cliff Vaughs at Hardy's shop in the bowels of L.A. Peter Fonda had met Hardy when Ben built the bike he rode in *The Wild Angels* a few years before *Easy Rider*. Although there *are* a few folks still around who dispute Hardy and Vaughs's exclusivity and/or wish to tweak it a bit.

Actor Dan Haggerty is also credited with having a hand in the creations.

And stunt rider Tex Hall.

And mechanic Larry Marcus.

And painter Dean Lanza.

The stickiness with the bike-building thickened down through the years because it always seemed like Hardy and Vaughs—both of whom are black—never received the recognition they should have for their part fabricating the two most recognized customs in history.

> Vaughs says the omission of his own name and that of other African-Americans in the retelling of the *Easy Rider* story is conspicuous.
>
> "Those bikes, when we talk about iconic, they are definitely iconic," he says. "But yet, the participation of Blacks…completely suppressed, completely suppressed. And I say suppressed, because no one talks about it."
>
> To this day, Vaughs has never watched *Easy Rider*. When asked why, he responds simply, "What for?"
>
> —Tom Dreisbach, National Public Radio, October 11, 2014

Vaughs has a strong point. Even in 2015 an online source offering a model of the Captain America bike was laying down that Fonda himself was part of the build team, accompanied solely by Haggerty and Hall.

> "The participation of Blacks…completely suppressed…."

"SOMEONE'S LAUGHING, LORD, KUMBAYA..."

Now, back to the obituaries.

It's more or less sort of generally accepted that before the filming of the movie was totally over, someone—or ones—stole the backup Captain America, the backup Billy bike, and the skidded-out Billy bike from a storage area. The blasted-in-half Captain America was apparently someplace else in pieces.

Things must have been not-surprisingly loose on the *Easy Rider* set, and at some point when the movie was wrapped, it was realized that the final campfire scene had not been filmed.

So, presumably, they all rolled another one and reloaded the cameras.

After the bikes had been stolen.

And that's why the Pans are not seen in the background as they were in the movie's other cannabis-kumbaya get-togethers.

So what happened after all of *that*?

Well, to this day, the stolen bikes have never been found. Given the climate of the times—people still building back-yarders piece by piece, swap meets that were really swap meets, not a ton of aftermarket stuff available, Pans still common—the consensus leans logically toward them being parted out.

As far as the wrecked Captain America goes, here's where things hitch a ride on a Roswell saucer and jet into Jimmy Hoffa land. Dennis Hopper would even comment from the grave.

Sources from books to newspapers to magazines to documentaries to websites to eyewitnesses have sworn to such "truths" as the following:

> The demolished bike was rebuilt by Dan Haggerty, sold at an
> auction in 2001, and now resides at the National Motorcycle
> Museum in Anamosa, Iowa.
> *Legendary Motorcycles: The Stories and Bikes Made Famous by Elvis,*
> *Peter Fonda, Kenny Roberts, and Other Motorcycling Greats*

> The burned bike was later restored by Peter Fonda and was sold to
> John Parham and can be seen in the National Motorcycle Museum
> in Anamosa Iowa.
> —IMDB and numerous classic movie sites

> I know for a fact that the leftover parts from *all* the Pans were
> thrown into the Venice canals.
> —A longtime SoCal biker who prefers to remain anonymous

The only remaining original "Captain America" Harley Davidson driven by Peter Fonda in *Easy Rider* was destroyed today [Dec. 13, 2010] along with other bikes and classic cars in a fire at a collector's warehouse in Austin, Texas. The cause of the fire at Gordon Granger's warehouse, which also claimed the first car owned by Tejano superstar Selena, has yet to be determined, but there's currently a dog sniffing around for gasoline or another accelerant....

—KXAN News, Austin, TX

After the filming, the wrecked bike was procured by actor Dan Haggerty, who began rebuilding it but never finished. It was then sold, the restoration being completed by Dave Ohrt.

—"Captain America: A Chopper Profile,"
by the Auto Editors of *Consumer Guide*

Now [in late 2014], the iconic stars-and-stripes Harley-Davidson is going up for auction, and is expected to fetch between $1 million-$1.2 million, because it is the only one which remains from filming.... The seller is Michael Eisenberg, a California businessman who once co-owned a Los Angeles motorcycle-themed restaurant with Fonda and *Easy Rider* costar Dennis Hopper. Mr. Eisenberg bought it last year from National Motorcycle Museum and Dan Haggerty.... The gleaming panhead chopper with chromed hardtail

Posters were ultra-groovy in the 1960s—from black-light Hendrix psychedelia to Jim Morrison's black-and-white angst to the Fillmore's far-out flyers—but none were more iconic than those that reared large with the *Easy Rider* choppers.

frame is accompanied by three letters of authenticity. One is signed by the National Motorcycle Museum, where it was displayed for 12 years. Another is from Fonda and a third from Haggerty.

—*Daily Mail*, September 17, 2014

DENNIS'S LONG-DISTANCE CALL

But from the grave, Hopper was apparently not a signatory on any of those letters.

Actor Michael Madsen was so outraged by our [*Los Angeles Times*] story on the auction sale of a motorcycle purportedly used in the filming of "Easy Rider" that he telephoned, from a movie set in Romania, to voice his concerns...

[Close friend, Dennis] Hopper, Madsen said, told him the whole story of making "Easy Rider" and what happened to the motorcycles used in filming it.

And the bike sold in Calabasas on Saturday night, for a whopping $1.62 million, including auction fees, isn't one of them, Madsen said.

"That thing they sold?" the gravel-voiced veteran actor said. "Dennis Hopper, from his grave, is telling you, through Michael Madsen, 'That ain't the Captain America bike.'..."

Hopper told [Madsen] the four bikes used in the making of "Easy Rider" had all been stolen or destroyed. Madsen said Hopper disputed the lurid story of how armed gunmen stole three of the motorcycles from "Easy Rider" stuntman Tex Hall, who, the story goes, later went hunting for the thieves with a machine gun.

"They were in a storage unit," Madsen said. "They got stolen, and sold for parts. They were never seen again. They don't exist."

Given all the questions about the "Captain America" motorcycle's provenance, why would anyone pay $1.62 million for it?

"Everyone wants to believe that's the bike," Madsen growled. "They're willing to pay $1 million to imagine that's the bike. That's kind of nostalgic and nice, but the truth is—it isn't...."

Madsen...said he heard the voice of Hopper telling him to set the record straight for anyone who thought the real Captain America bike had been sold—or was out there waiting to be sold....

"As I sit here in Romania, I heard his voice in the sky. [Madsen] said, 'Michael, please, tell them.'"

—Charles Fleming, *Los Angeles Times*, October 21, 2014

If anyone could jump that ethereal plane, the space-cowboy Hopper has a good chance. But the truth from the confusion is that these four bikes are the subject of more myths, mysteries, and rumors than anything else on two wheels that has ever rolled in or out of the biker culture. Ultimately, they seem to have been scattered—in various ways—to the wild and wicked winds.

And that could easily be their most fitting fate, considering that trying to live free as a breeze is exactly what this movie was all about.

You, yourself, may even be a part of this cycle circle of life.

If you own a Pan, then maybe you are sharing some parts purloined from the *Easy Rider* bikes. And that's cool; the statute of limitations on receiving stolen goods is probably long over for you and, in a personal sense, it's kind of like having your favorite saint's bone-relic on a bedroom altar, a brother's ashes mixed into your paint, or a vial of your lover's blood on a chain around your neck.

But if you've ever shelled out upwards of two mil for the absolute, one hundred percent bona fide, gen-u-ine, letter-of-authenticity-fied, chromed-out Cap'n 'Merica Pan, well you might just find yourself with a combination of your financial advisers *and* Dennis Hopper's ghost on your ass.

REACTION AND RESPONSE

It doesn't look like we'll ever know, dog. Hardy and Vaughs were definitely the main builders, but other hands claim to have held a tool or two. And the bikes: well, three of them seem to have been divided up like the booty in a rich uncle's will, hopefully spreading some tasty slices of the pie to a lot of the family. The fourth Pan has become the object of unending legal and legend-sure debates that transcend life itself.

PART VI

Celebrity

193

CHAPTER 25:

"DIDN'T ANYONE CHECK HER ID?"

THE AWKWARD-EST ISSUE OF *EASYRIDERS*

INTERROGATING THE SUBJECT

Did *Easyriders* really feature an underage chick in one of their nudie spreads? Are these still in circulation?

Be good or don't get caught.

—Traci Lords

Magazines helped to build this culture and the image.

In the '60s and '70s, some counterculture young folks—and even some who were starting to age—were reading and absorbing *Rolling Stone, Tiger Beat, CREEM, 16* magazine, the *Free Press*, and other inner-social-music statements of the time. On another side of the long-hair fence were those searching the newsstands for *Colors, Big Bike*, and—starting in June of 1971—*Easyriders* magazine.

Boots and sandals sometimes mixed, but more often than not, they didn't. Such was the strange dichotomy that commonly included sex, drugs, rock 'n' roll, and long hair but broke *un*commonly when subjects turned to the power of motorcycle clubs versus the happy electrical-banana-peeling back of the passive hippie culture.

The fall 1970 issue of *Colors* included articles titled "Outlaws & Drugs" and "The Angry Man" and a news column called Exhaust Fumes. A *Rolling Stone* issue released at about the same time was calling America in the 1970s a "Pitiful Helpless Giant" and featured pieces about George Harrison and radical left-wing poet Allen Ginsberg— "America, I've given you all and now I'm nothing."

Chopped Panheads and peace-signed Volkswagen microbuses were very different vehicles headed in very different directions.

ON THE COVER OF THE *ROLLING STONE*

So, as years rambled by, everyone gravitated toward what they liked best.

Groovy, bitchin', and fuckin' A! That's what America is all about.

A lot of those magazines—and the people who devoured them—are still around, some a bit more dog eared than others. *Rolling Stone* now leans even more toward politics, although they're still liable to cover something like "the latest progressive percussionist in hip-hop fusion." But Dr. Hook & the Medicine Show probably aren't going to be on the cover again anytime soon.

On the biker side of the rack, *Colors, Big Bike, Outlaw Biker*, and most others are long gone.

Not *Easyriders*.

The glossy motorcycle monthly never seems to run out of gas, but the octane has been lowered. *Easyriders* understood the clout of the clubs. The magazine covered trials, fed intrusions, MCs suing local law enforcement agencies, and many of their runs. Old issues, along with the mag's 1980s and 1990s video series, are billet-bright booty, shining

The very first issue of *Easyriders*, "For the Swinging Biker." The article about "Rock Stars and their Choppers" featured a Rich Budelier–built Sporty owned by Red Shepard, one of the West Coast stars of *Hair*: "Star of the tribal love-rock musical Hair freaks the straights as he flashes through Hollywood on his Sportster." *Archives of Bill Hayes*

in a vast treasure trove of reference for anyone who wants to understand the history of this lifestyle.

But, like Dwight Yokam says, "Baby, things change..."

The first issue of *Easyriders* contained "Who slipped Superman the acid" and "Designed for wasted chicks?" Recent cover stories have included "Guide to Tools and Lubricants," "June Bug Boogie," and "Columbus Showdown: Bike Show Finale."

Pictures of patches or club info?

All of that appears to have dissolved into the silicone of the centerspread chicks' boobs.

"GIRL YOU KNOW IT'S TRUE"

Nothing, however, can throw camp-dirt on the fire that was *Easyriders*. Spending some time with a classic issue is truly a Biker 101 course in all that anyone with a bike should know.

MCs, early builders, pioneers, legendary runs, laws, law fights, the beginnings of bikers rights' organizations, readers' naked old ladies, bad jokes, good jokes, and backyard put-togethers were all there between original covers, right along with the club coverage. Expensive torpedo tits and trailered no-ride mega-money customs weren't ever listed in those prehistoric TOCs.

Within each magazine's niche, both the hippies' *Rolling Stone* and the bikers' *Easyriders* have survived. But while *RS* was looking ahead at covering Milli Vanilli's Grammy for best new artist—one of the biggest deceptions in music history—*Easyriders* was already releasing the classic issue of all classics, featuring an "oops!" that ironically would be right there with Milli Vanilli singing "Girl You Know It's True."

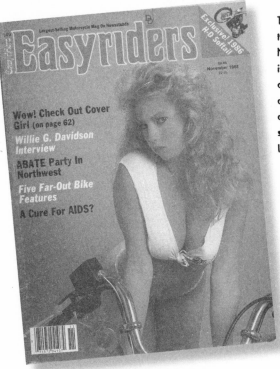

The titillating yet tasteful, tied-up-in-legal-bondage November '85 *Easyriders* issue that featured "Susie"—a cute handle for the lovely and talented but somewhat age-confused "adult film" scene stealer extraordinaire, Traci Lords. *Archives of Bill Hayes*

MANN FIRST

When subscribers and newsstand purchasers of the November 1985 issue of *Easyriders* got their copies, it was pleasure-business as usual. The cover blurbed, "Willie G. Davidson Interview," "ABATE Party In Northwest," "Five Far-Out Bike Features," and "Wow! Check Out Cover Girl (on page 62)."

Okay, let's see what's inside. As always, the Dave Mann centerpiece was a highlight, and nighttime was Mann's setting for this issue's work.

Two rigid shovels lead a nighttime pack in front of the Harbor Lights Bar under a shadowy suspension bridge that could be in 'Frisco or San Pedro or anywhere in the imaginations that Mann was so expert at stirring.

Turn the page.

PROBLEMS ON PAGE 62

The rest of the issue is even more of a textbook of the times: coverage of the funeral of the legendary Chocolate George, the most politically *in*correct cure for AIDS ever, hand-built customs, an "Ol' Lady Contest" with contestants who hadn't yet waltzed into the waxing age, and much more aberrant antiquity.

But that "Wow!" on page 62 was indeed a "wow."

And an "Uh-oh!"

On page 62 was "Susie" on a 1986 FXST: "Hardbelly On A Softail."

It was a pretty damn impressive four-page spread of a very cute chick on a bike that was very much secondary in the scenery. There were detailed stats and descriptions— about her: "The FOXY Hardbelly has time-honored biker-bitch styling and the latest V-TWAT™ technology."

A teeny weeny problem, however, occurs here in those fleshy four pages. It busts out when one analyzes the math that sizes up that November 1985 "Hardbelly."

"Susie" turned out to be "actress" Traci Lords, born May 7, 1968. Her beyond-jail-bait eighteenth birthday would not be celebrated until the supple springtime of 1986.

Now, taking into consideration that issues of *Easyriders* are released a few months before their cover date, and back things up even more to the photo session when those photos for the November '85 issue were, uh, snatched...well, you have a Susie who is, uh...you see...uh...hmm...really, really *young*!

"But, boss, her ID said..."

"THE OVERSIZE NIPPLES ARE STANDARD..."

Straight up, *Easyriders* got punked.

But they weren't alone.

Traci would go down (no pun intended) in hardcore history as one of the most mythic, mysterious, and rumored "adult film" stars on the planet. In late May of 1986, three weeks after her long-in-coming eighteenth birthday, authorities finally discovered that Miss Lords had used an ID from a stolen identity to make a buttload of porno films, as well as to do plenty of other memorable "modeling" for magazines—including *Penthouse*—while underage.

Things got messy quick. Messier even than the floor of the set during the filming of her first flick, *What Gets Me Hot!* The owners of her movie agency were arrested, and distributors pulled films, VHS tapes, promo photos, and everything else with even the slightest scent of her on it, at a cost loss of millions—prosecution for trafficking in kiddie porn doesn't ever look good on a business résumé. Lords's case is still considered the biggest scandal to penetrate the porn industry.

And it's still a little creepy in the biker universe, too. *Easyriders'* "spread" may have been an innocent slip-up in the vetting-of-the-vixen department, but the fact remains that the world's premier biker magazine put a boot very deep into its mouth as it sold its "technical description" of an extremely young girl: "And the list goes on: The oversize nipples are standard, and the rib cage and hip bones have been reinforced for a more solid ride."

Good solid specs, guys. At least no one mentioned anything about a custom kidskin seat.

Recently, on eBay, the "entire set" of *Easyriders* magazines for 1985 was offered at auction.

Except, of course, for the November issue.

REACTION AND RESPONSE

It's a limp exercise to argue with hard mathematics. And according to the numbers, *Easyriders* indeed featured one of the most iconic of all porn stars at her young and youthful best. And other than the possibility of a few issues stashed away in Jared Fogle's closet, the tainted November 1985 issue of the mag is as rare as a twelve-inch Subway Spicy Italian in a federal pen.

CHAPTER 26:

WHO REALLY HATCHED EASY RIDER?

"SOMEONE'S" INTELLECTUAL PROPERTY CHANGED A GENERATION

INTERROGATING THE SUBJECT

After all these years, it seems like more and more myths, mysteries, and rumors keep riding with the ghosts of Wyatt and Billy. Who came up with the "outta sight" idea for this "far out" movie anyway? Fonda? Hopper? Or was it someone else?

We've frisked the mysteries of the scooters. Now we'll pat down the myths and rumors behind the story—and in many ways, it's a stumble into an even soupier fog.

"It's a real freak-out, man!"

The "true story" of the origin of *Easy Rider* is most perfectly told in the most perfect of all '60s settings: San Francisco. From the Tenderloin District to the upscale world of Mill Valley and the home of a prominent media star, "Whose idea was it?" is as purple-hazy as "What happened to the bikes?"

But there is a bridge—not the Golden Gate, the Bay, or the Dumbarton, but a connective human cast that can tie together the open ends of a generation and the rambling roots of an immortal movie that "went looking for America, but couldn't find it anywhere."

AND APPEARING AS THEMSELVES ARE...

Fonda and Hopper, of course.

Peter Coyote.

Bill Fritsch.

Coyote is the author of *Sleeping Where I Fall*, probably the definitive narrative of the excessive highs and lows of the 1960s. He was one of the famous "Diggers" of Haight-Ashbury. His Renaissance man persona includes actor, author, and biker.

Fritsch, a.k.a. "Sweet William" and "Tumbleweed," was a motorcycle club member in the clusterfumble core of the '60s. He was at Altamont when the blood spilled. He was shot in Fresno while selling cocaine during a house party organized to raise money for the African Student Movement, leaving him with permanent paralysis of one side of his body and a bullet still lodged in his brain.

But hard history is the most genuine bestower of title, and Sweet William sure as hell earned his status as a legitimate legend. With or without a club patch, with or without the ability to ride or even walk un-hunched or un-hobbled, he was mythic and marvelous. Even when he wound up living alone in a small room, dealing with his paralysis and memories in the bottom-side of "The City."

He paid a steep price for the life he led, but so do a lot of people—people who never *really* live.

A HEAVY SUPPORTING CAST

"The *Easy Rider* Germination Controversy" is how Fritsch referred to the "Whose idea was it?" question. It was a good way to put it; a lot of crooked-row social stuff was being heavily fertilized and germinating in the late '60s, and the Bay Area bred some of the most bountiful harvests.

In 1967, Eric Burdon and his Animals released their *Winds of Change* album. The cut "San Franciscan Nights" provided a better panorama of The City than even the lookout point at Treasure Island. Burdon's trip through 'Frisco's mind-melting pot of old and young, love and beauty, cops and hippies—*and* its bikers—celebrated a one-off mix that set trends and sideswiped much of society-past.

The mix also comingled and coalesced—to an extent.

It was that free flow that brought Peter Coyote's group of counterculture think-tankers, the Diggers, into the arms and hearts of Hollywood stars, where an association with the "latest" in everything is a lifestyle imperative.

AND NOW, CENTER STAGE...

The counterculture's paradoxical embracing of motorcycle clubs was another part of the free progressive flow. The overall community that resulted from all the intermelding had a lot in common, with everyone enjoying the day's cool collective of sex, drugs, and rock 'n' roll.

They also had shared enemies, usually in the form of "straights" and unhip cutthroat capitalists and authorities. In Los Angeles, some money-hungry artistry-last music producers tried to stage an event using the Diggers' name and aura. According to Coyote, he and Sweet William, along with a "couple of others," headed south to straighten things out.

Which they did.

But that trip would lead to much more than just another eating of the establishment's lunch.

In *Sleeping Where I Fall*, Coyote explains in detail how the group was invited to stay at the house of Benny Shapiro, the manager of hippiedom's favorite sitar slinger, Ravi Shankar. Peter Fonda, Dennis Hopper, and actor Brandon deWilde would join them. Right up there with the sex, drugs, and rock 'n' roll was artistic expression—an exercise often generated by any or all of the prior three. Shapiro's place was paradise for a brainstorming of ideas for producing the ultimate film.

You can almost hear one of Ravi's mystical ragas as Coyote presents Fritsch in Shakespearean glory, laying down *his* thoughts:

Then Sweet William took the floor, magnificent in his [club] colors, his hard-chiseled face and poetic eyes mesmerizing even those of us who knew him well.

"You know what I'd do?" he said, "I'd make a movie about me and a buddy just riding around. Just going around the country doing what we do, seeing what we see, you know. Showing the people what things are like."

"Well said, old mole . . . !"
"Showing the people what things are like" might just make for a far-out flick.

NOT-SO-QUIET ON THE SET

Where the actual name for the film came from is another of the shadow stories. One of the most colorful theories wades out of that *other* controversy about who built the bikes:

> It was Cliff [Vaughs, who built the Pans along with Ben Hardy] who actually first offered the name "Easy Rider" to Fonda. It was a term he used in the day. What's an Easy Rider? That depends on who you ask. In the 1900s it meant a freeloader, a guy who mooched off you. To Dennis Hopper, it meant a man who lived off the money of a whore. He got it from an old Mae West movie. Whatever Cliff meant by it, I'm not sure. All I know is he redefined the word.
> —MrZip66.com, 2012

So one way or another, *Easy Rider* now had a theme and a title. But it also had some trouble. Again, according to Coyote—and the Bible—the love of money rooted its way into a little bit of evil.

Fonda and Hopper were running with the idea of the movie; it was going to happen. Coyote was asked to participate by featuring his San Francisco Mime Troupe, who would write, direct, and perform in a segment of the film. But a compensatory offer of just twenty dollars a week for himself, a "place on Fonda's couch," and nothing for the troupe didn't work for Coyote. Even with pleas that leaned on the film's low budget and the importance of social statement versus commercial venture, the Digger stood firm as Fonda and Hopper rode on.

When *Easy Rider* hit the theaters, however, the segment intended for the San Francisco Mime Troupe was there. Coyote's troupe had called themselves "guerrilla theater"; the troupe in the film was identified as "Gorilla Theater."

That wasn't cool, man . . . that just wasn't cool.

ROLL THE CREDITS

Memories of the *Easy Rider* Germination Controversy must have freewheeled their way in and out of Sweet William's mind, yet it really seemed that—after so long—it didn't bother him much. He'd give a one-shouldered shrug when asked about any grudges he may still have concerning his idea being "borrowed."

Maybe that's because it wasn't just an idea; it was *him*. Anyone can borrow (or steal) a concept, but no one can live another's life.

Especially one like William Fritsch lived.

REACTION AND RESPONSE

While several from the "mind-melting pot" of 1960s counterculture had obvious influence, Peter Coyote makes it pretty damn clear that William Fritsch vocalized the lifestyle-essence of *Easy Rider*. His "showing the people what things are like" statement is classic, epitomizing the aggressive open art of the times. William "Sweet William" "Tumbleweed" Fritsch passed away in a San Francisco nursing home on March 14, 2015.

"Will the real Captain America bike please put your kickstand up?!" It seems like lots of garages and museums have one—but nobody, except maybe for Dennis Hopper's ghost, knows for sure which is the real rebuilt deal!
Bill Hayes and Jennifer Thomas

CHAPTER 27:

WHO'S LAUGHING NOW?

THE MYSTERY OF THE MOST HATED
BIKER TELEVISION SHOW IN HISTORY

INTERROGATING THE SUBJECT

Was *The Devils Ride* absolutely the most vilified media biker
production of any type or genre? *Ever*? If so, why?

So far *The Devils Ride* seems to have offended a majority of motorcyclists and television enthusiasts in this hemisphere, from real live bikers to Hollywood producers. The show is not just bad. Actual people have been damaged by it. It is impossible to putt through San Diego County on a Saturday afternoon without bumping into a dozen men who have been damaged in one way or another.

—AgingRebel.com, June 24, 2012

P remiering on May 8, 2012 on the Discovery Channel, *The Devils Ride* paralleled—at least for a few seasons—*Sons of Anarchy*. But apparently to viewers, *TDR* wasn't quite as charming as *SOA*.

Discovery's marketing claimed their offering would "take you inside the world of motorcycle clubs"—also the implied goal of *SOA*. But these shows were definitely not the same. Just a quick example: *SOA* featured superstar Charlie Hunnam as "Jax"; *The Devils Ride* gave us "Snubz" as himself.

But the first mystery surrounding *The Devils Ride* was an issue that was never in question for *Sons*. Everyone—well, almost everyone...a few thirty-something bloggers living in their moms' basements failed to catch on—knew that the Sons of Anarchy was a fictional club. But in the beginning, especially in areas far from SoCal, a lot of confusion coagulated as to whether or not the centerpiece MC on *The Devils Ride,* the Laffing Devils, was fact or crap. Was this production an actual camera-in-your-face documentary, a reality show, a docudrama, an *SOA*-like serial soap opera, or a fractured combination of all four?

> The premiere of the new Discovery Channel reality series, "The Devils Ride," has created quite a stir among viewers, raising one question in particular: Is this a real club, or one created specifically for television?...Some are adamant that the show could not be real; others are taking a more open approach, giving the show—and the Laffing Devils—a chance to prove themselves.
> —Mechele R. Dillard, huliq.com, May 15, 2012

Waiting for that "proving" wouldn't take long.

BRING ON THE CLOWNS

Comments sped through social media. This one, in response to the huliq.com blurb, was indicative of the majority's "exit polling":

> What respectable MC airs their MC business with the world on national television? Also, if you listen and watch what goes on in the first airing, they contradict themselves relative to membership/ tension, etc. Lastly, the wives of the members go out for dinner in public with cameras rolling for national TV and they (or Prospect Charles) worry about some paparazzi taking pics of them? If you don't want your pic taken, why are you on TV? Also, I wonder if they realize that [their color combination] is the colors of another well known worldwide MC that has been around for over 50 years. I am curious to know if these TV bikers got permission to use those two colors and center logo from the worldwide MC that owns them?

But the anonymity and banter of social media wasn't nearly as strong as what was being said on the streets of the real world.

> This thing [*The Devils Ride*] is really worse than even *Gangland* and all those hit-piece documentaries. And that's mainly because it really makes bikers all look like clowns. *Gangland* and all that shit makes us look like bad guys but damn, at the end of the day that's better than looking like fucking clowns.
>> —An anonymous biker overheard bitching at a bar

MORE CLOWNS CLIMB OUT OF THE LITTLE CAR

Along with the speeding comments from viewers came the quick-churning realization that the club did indeed exist.

Real news—and some real legal ugliness—was being made apart from the show.

The "paparazzi" mentioned in the old ladies' dinner debacle turned out to be a professional photographer who just happened to be passing by that evening in the touristy Gaslamp section of San Diego, where the show and the club are centered.

He saw the women, saw the television camera crew, and with that instinctive journalistic opportunism figured he'd take some shots of something that just might turn out to be interesting.

It did.

But not in the way he'd hoped.

208 CHAPTER 27

As he started to snap a shot or two, he claims that he was pushed from behind, taken to the ground, and eventually had five men and women associated with the club beating him. He ended up broken: a broken nose, a broken cheekbone, broken ribs, and a broken ankle. And he received no real help from the cops he, himself, had to call (no one else seemed to have the energy to 9-1-1 their cells) after hobbling away from the scene on his one good foot.

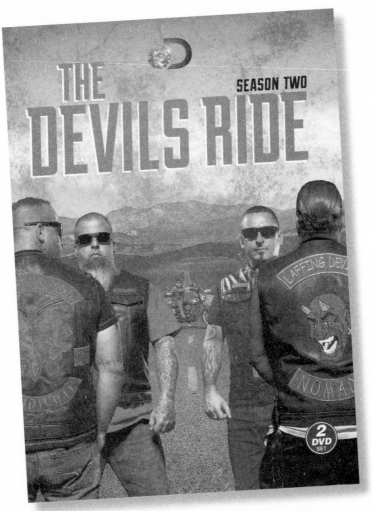

In first run, the show lasted for a just few seasons of pissing people off, but the DVDs are out there forever, apparently continuing to make friends and influence people.

After he got out of his hospital bed, the bloodied photog headed for court. He sued everybody—not just for the attack but for airing footage of the brawl without his permission.

In the case against the restaurant, the photographer alleged that the owners "invited *Devils Ride* filmmakers into the bar on the night of January 27, 2012, so cast members could provoke fights with members of the public for the reality show."

If that was true, well, it sure did the trick. But was it good TV, or was it as lame as yet another of those golden Sean Penn–Kanye West–Kardashian Clown Crew get-outta-my-face moments? The kind of thing that's more at home in the giddiness of gossip columns than in the inner-circle operations of a legitimate motorcycle club?

TOUGH GUYS IN TWITTER WARS

The rest of 2012 produced more heat for the Devils.

In May, a lone member of another (well established) MC got into a fight with two Devils and an "associate." The single club guy was charged with four felonies and five gang enhancements. The Laffing Devils were not charged.

A collective of MCs in the area put on fundraisers for the lone guy's legal costs, but that didn't stop SWAT from conducting a dawn raid on his house—a raid that produced nothing in the way of evidence for anything.

Two days after Christmas, the Devils' "Sandman" felt some legal flames of his own.

> ### "Devils Ride" Star BUSTED for Burglary and Stabbing
> Discovery Channel's "The Devils Ride"—a reality show about a San Diego biker gang—has some real deal bad dudes...because TMZ has learned, one of the stars just got arrested for stabbing a guy while burglarizing his house.
>
> According to docs, "Sandman"—real name Robert Johnston—was arrested on December 27 for burglary, attempted murder (with a knife), assault with a deadly weapon and making criminal threats.
>
> In charging documents, prosecutors say Sandman broke into the victim's house on Dec. 22 with the intent to commit burglary, and at some point, stabbed the victim...inflicting "great bodily injury."
>
> Sandman is still behind bars, being held on $755,000 bail.
>
> —TMZ, January 7, 2013

Then things got *really* scary when *The Devils Ride* executive producer Jason Hervey got into a Twitter war with *SOA* kingpin Kurt Sutter. According to the *International Business Times*, Hervey tweeted that "Moses is to the Israelites as Kurt Sutter is to motorcycle clubs."

Sutter counter-tweeted things that brought into question *TDR's* brains and brawn, calling Hervey (who played Wayne Arnold on *The Wonder Years*) "fat" and offering to "buy all the Devils chocolate valentine hearts. Their feelings are so hurt."

Twitter may now have replaced parking lots and back alleys as the ultimate bloody battleground.

MEANWHILE, BACK ON THE SET

While the outside legal entanglements were getting more and more snarled up, the inside drama on the show was dripping and thick. Intra- and inter-club personality conflicts were storming, and war was a-brewin' between the Devils and a hostile spin-off MC called the Sinister Mob Syndicate, complete with a major officer named "Rockem"!

More business as usual while the cameras were rolling.

But then, loyal devotees were left cliff-hanging by their fingernails in early 2014:

> Last night, fans watched as the ultimatum given to the Laffing
> Devils and Sin Mob was played out in the desert on the Season
> Finale of "The Devils Ride." But, could it have actually been the
> Series Finale for the show?
> —TVRuckus.com, March 11, 2014

The mystery of the ultimatum may never be solved!
What would happen next?
Would anything happen next?

"HAVE A CIGAR, BOY ... "

What happened next was a deep breath and a look around, kind of like what happens in the silence following a head-on car crash on a lonely rural road when no one seems to be moving, steam is wafting up from busted radiators, and the only witness—an old, slow-shuffling field farmer—is too stunned to even talk. Or at the election-night campaign headquarters of a politician who just got eaten alive by twenty-three percentage points. The band has packed up early, shiny rally posters are now debris, and a once-happy hall is litter scattered and empty—what the hell just occurred here?

The Devils Ride was a mess. It reduced the motorcycle-club culture to that of the WWE; all that was left was to replace black leather and beer with yellow tights and steroids. It made a mockery of sacred MC codes by making it seem okay to air club business to the world and pissed off a lot of people.

And for what?

In June 2012, right in the middle of the show's crazy-train runaway, a show-featured LDMC member—a guy who identified himself as "Hawkster"—posted a long comment online. Regardless of the unbelievably bad judgment that infested this show from the top down, his laments should serve as a warning for clubs or biker-connected individuals who get tempted by those "have a cigar, boy" types of media promises:

> The club was founded Dec. 2006, members of the local C.O.C. (Confederation of Clubs) and trademarked Laffing Devils MC in 2010... Four years ago the Devils were approached by a film company with the idea (for the show). They (the producers) made a three-minute promo DVD to send to the networks. Time went by and no one seemed interested and it was all but forgotten. Last summer, Discovery Channel came a calling and they started filming last fall... People think there was a lot of money in it for The Devils, but in fact, it was peanuts after it was divided up. It is a fact that Tommy (a booted-out member) took off with as much as he could get his hands on and whatever side deals he had made with them... The bottom line is, The Devils were told they would be portrayed as who and what they really were and nothing more, or we wouldn't [*sic*] have thought twice about doing it... After seeing the first advertisements for "The Devils Ride," we knew we were fucked...
>
> —"Hawkster," AgingRebel.com, June 15, 2012

Okay.

A lot of folks have been buggered by the media. People clamor "Give us dirty laundry!" and there are plenty of outlets ready and willing to let them smell the stench. But this danger is no secret; all the more reason to be on guard in this jungle.

LAST LAUGH

One final Laff on the Devils comes back to that old, old adage: "Things can always be worse."

> [T]he founder of The Laffing Devils, Tommy "Gypsy" Quinn, apparently sold them out to the Discovery Channel after being booted from the club for marrying a cop. The Laffing Devils have since disbanded and Gypsy "was arrested on August 29, 2012 regarding allegations of lewd acts on a minor child. San Diego television news station and Fox affiliate KSWB-TV reported that Tommy Quinn was arrested on suspicion of having his minor step-daughter perform oral sex on him at least six times." So, there's your

"brotherhood" and the "real man" who founded it.

None of that is in the show. In fact, Gypsy unceremoniously disappeared from the program after his 2012 arrest.

—TheMerryMonk.com, November 20, 2013

A lot of creative projects and the people behind them get bad reviews, but damn, this one represents a new high in lows. Nothing on television or the movies—including *Gangland*, the various butcher-the-bikers documentaries, *SOA*, or even *Chopper Chicks in Zombietown* ever skinned senses alive like *The Devils Ride* did.

Motorcycle clubs are a different kind of rodeo when it comes down to how the spectacle is portrayed and displayed. No one genuine in this lifestyle wants to be considered a "fucking clown."

REACTION AND RESPONSE

Yes, *The Devils Ride* was, in fact, the most hated biker production ever! When critical comments and reviews become pure word-on-the-street venom, you know your creation has hit a very short nerve. Creepy clowns are never cool.

CHAPTER 28:

CONFESSIONS TO MURDER ON NATIONAL TELEVISION?

HMM...IF I'M NOT MISTAKEN, THERE'S NO STATUTE OF LIMITATIONS ON THAT

INTERROGATING THE SUBJECT

Did the History Channel's *Gangland* really feature an on-air confession to nearly forty homicides?

Bummer. That's worse than the director yelling "Cut!" But damn, bro, if you have felony warrants out for your arrest, maybe you shouldn't be on TV. Every television show and all computer-connected media today is forever. Nothing that goes out there is ever going to go away, although maybe you will.

AN "ACCIDENTAL" BEHEADING

And then there was the 2015 macabre mystery case of zillionaire Robert Durst. His first wife suddenly disappeared in 1982, and one of his closest friends was found dead in her home in 2000—but no charges were brought against Durst even though all the slaying signs pointed his way. Then in 2003, he convinced a jury that his admitted shooting and dismemberment of a neighbor was an "accident." The neighbor's head was never found.

Durst looked untouchable for all these missteps until a 2015 six-part HBO documentary, *The Jinx: The Life and Deaths of Robert Durst*, prompted Bob D. to talk a bit too much, and shoveled up and showcased other evidence against him in prior killings. He was arrested in New Orleans not long after the cable conviction.

And he's not alone.

Parole jumpers on weekly lottery spins, deadbeat dads on afternoon judge shows, narcissistic nuts talking about their crimes on social media—a lot of people have exposed themselves, seduced by quick fame in the flat-screen universe. Unfortunately for them, many have experienced very unhappy endings.

It happens in the biker world, too. But one of the most mysterious two-wheeled tip-offs produced consequences that *didn't* happen.

CHOOSING A CAST FROM THE STOOL–PIGEON POOL

Beginning in 2007 and spanning seven seasons, eighty-seven episodes, and endless reruns, the History Channel's *Gangland* performed living autopsies on all sorts of urban-intense fraternal orders. From skinheads to the KKK to the Crips to Oklahoma City's South Side Locos, *Gangland* skewered everyone with a tattoo and a tribe.

Also included on the show's menu were bitter exposés of eleven top-tier motorcycle clubs; a few were even given from two to four episodes of dedicated destruction. The quantity didn't matter. Virtually all the episodes were stamped out from the same terrible template that utilized seven simple rules of ruin:

- Go to the stoolie pool and sign out a pissed-off ex-member, a cop, an infiltrator, or an entire chorus line that includes them all.

- Hide them in spooky shadows and/or shroud them in a Charles Dickens signature model Ghost of Christmas Yet to Come hood.

- Use voice distortion to make them all sound like the lead singer in Slayer as they growl and chirp out whatever incriminating and libelous things they want, under the cover of anonymity.

- Cut away to the same few newspaper headlines and press photos of alleged crimes over and over and over.

- Cut away to loops of the same stock film footage over and over and over.

- Go heavy on "reenactments" and "dramatizations" of events to make them look exactly, one hundred percent perfectly, like they probably went down.

- Under all of that, roll gritty narration by the same kind of voice that hawks on trailers for movies such as *Saw: The Final Chapter* in 3-D: "The traps come alive!"

In the formula-predictability department, all that was missing was a laugh track.

"VIEWER DISCRETION IS ADVISED"—FOR A LOT OF REASONS

"Snitch Slaughter" was the title of the *Gangland* episode that victimized the Vagos MC. First aired on November 5, 2009, it was the series' longest stretch in the low points of credibility.

It followed the template perfectly, but three specific hits produced mystifying misses.

One was the introduction of a guy named "Lonesome." The viewers are told that good ol' Lonesome was an "associate" of the Vagos. He goes on and on about how the club recruited him to "handle business" and to "do things." Then the Vagos "promoted" him "from thief to assassin."

"You want someone whacked," he said, "he's fuckin' dead. No problem."

But as the show goes on it's discovered that, *gasp!*, Lonesome is a snitch—he's an informant for the feds.

Who has "whacked" people while on the job?!

Isn't that in the "things you can't do" section of the undercover cop manual?

So the intro as a current club "associate" is bogus, and the idea that he's tied to the feds while "whacking" around is as hard to swallow as shoe polish strained through cheap white bread.

And, not to be mean, but the way this guy is made up, he looks a lot like Travolta in *Wild Hogs*.

No wonder he's lonesome.

About three-quarters of the way through the episode, black-and-white surveillance footage of two members planning a "hit" is aired. The recording was allegedly made by a camera placed under the dashboard of one of their cars.

Talk into the ashtray, please...

In the videoed conversation, one supposed member (with a pixelated face) jokes about the fact that the club is really a "gang," not a club—feeding RICO-like LEO appetites.

No mention is made of who hooked up the bug or how the camera was placed. Or how no one—in a culture where such things are not easily disguised—noticed something like that hanging from the dashboard *of their own car*.

But the show's real kicker was the continuing banter from "Sniper."

"Sniper"—perfectly darkened by the Dickens duds and with a voice ready to belt out "Raining Blood"—was introduced as a Vagos member. But the producers must have figured that viewers have short memories, because by the end of the episode he was reintroduced as a former member who had been out for a few years.

In between those two toss-ups of the truth, Sniper spent a lot of time describing all the murders he committed for the club. He talked about bullets to the head, body disappearance by acid bath, grinding up skulls, feeding flesh to crows, and an eventual straight-up admission to being responsible for "between thirty-five and thirty-eight murders"—murder being a crime that has no statute of limitations.

Now, cops were also featured on the show. So...you would've thought that someone might have at least said something.

Or brought out the handcuffs.

Hell, that poor bastard in the Ohio commercial got the big pinch for grand theft—small-potatoes, video-game kind of stuff compared to almost forty *murders*!

But then again, this is *Gangland*: "The insider story of some of America's most notorious street gangs."

Really?

REACTION AND RESPONSE

Yep! "Sniper" spilled the bloody beans about his dozens of murders in front of God and everybody. But was it the truth, a "reenactment," a "dramatization," or an out-and-out lie? Somehow, the apparent lack of action by law enforcement narrows down the answer.

CHAPTER 29:

"HERE'S YOUR BIKES; OH, HEY, CAN YOU GUYS RIDE?"

GIVING THE CAST OF *SOA* THEIR KEYS

INTERROGATING THE SUBJECT

All right, just one more look into SOA—that's it! Did a Harley dealer actually work out a deal to customize personal "club-type" bikes for the cast so that they could "walk the walk" and not seem so much like actors? And could any of them really ride? Do any of them still ride?

W e're going to take just one more ride with the Sons of Anarchy.
We'll take that ride on the new bikes they received at the beginning of the
show's second season, a season when details were being considered a little
more closely. Always-on-her-bike photographer and writer Felicia Morgan
was there when the boys were handed their keys.

THE PROPER TOOL FOR THE PROPER JOB

Having spent much time in the NorCal area, Felicia was totally in tune with the
stomping-grounds setting of *SOA*. And having spent much time in the saddle of a big
bike, she was totally in tune with the machines that would be the personal putts of the
men of mayhem.

This exercise would be the ultimate in a spurring of "method acting."

"Supposedly based in California's central valley," our loyal-local tells us, "modeled
on the real town of Lodi, some speculate, our imaginary gunrunning bike club operates
from the fictitious town of Charming, which is anything but.

"In 2008, some 5.2 million viewers caught each episode of the first season, much
to the surprise of the show's execs who weren't expecting the series to even be noticed.
Season one on DVD and Blu-ray reportedly sold out in Lodi, Stockton, and other
surrounding valley towns in less than two hours after it was recently released."

Hooray for those hometown heroes!

Felicia goes on to report:

> Ed Morga, then general manager of Eagle's Nest Harley-Davidson
> in Lathrop, California, is one of the show's fans. But like many of
> us, Morga was bothered by the lack of reality in little details that
> screamed at him from his television.
>
> Working at a dealership that customizes bikes for a broad base
> of customers, including a few club members, Morga knows a thing
> or two about what club members ride. So Ed made some calls, and
> next thing he knew he was knee-deep in actors' agents, TV execs,
> and lawyers wrestling with his proposal to provide the cast with

personally customized Harley-Davidson motorcycles that would be more becoming to patched-out bikers.

He figured that if these guys could have bikes of their own to ride on their off time, they could more easily learn how to "walk the walk" that would make them appear more real on screen.

Over the span of five months, Morga and his right-hand man, Tommy Loredo, managed to arrange for cast members to place specific orders for brand-new Harley FXD Dynas and for each actor to be assigned his own personal mechanic to do creative customizing.

The great reward came when the actors traveled from SoCal up to Lathrop to meet their mechanics and get a first glance as well as a maiden lap around the dealership on their new wheels as fans looked on. The dealership was mobbed. An estimated seven thousand NorCal riders cruised out to meet their favorite pretend biker. People went nuts. Several women decided, in true biker fashion, that the best way to get a man's attention was to flash some flesh. As the actors signed autographs and posed for photos, bare breasts were pressed against windowpanes, and motocops tried in vain to control the huge clusterfuck in the roadway out front.

It was mayhem!

ONLY ONE OF THE BEACH BOYS EVER SURFED...

Felicia then circulated amongst the cast that was getting fully exposed to strange boobs and new bikes.

"One more bill of fare for the event was the attendance of Kurt Sutter, *SOA's* writer/producer, who also plays 'Big Otto' Delaney in the series," Felicia said.

> Charlie Hunnam was also there. He plays "Jax," of course, the official heartthrob of the show, and was the one who caused the wardrobe malfunctions for several rabid female fans. "Opie" was there, played by long and lean Ryan Hurst, as well as mohawked-and-head-tatted "Juice," Theo Rossi. Mark Boone, who plays "Bobby Elvis," rode as a teenager and, having now taken it back up, talked about his latest motorcycle crash and the repairs his bike required afterward.
>
> For my taste, the remaining bad boys of the cast are the only ones who come close to being riders off-set. "Chibs" is played by Tommy Flanagan, who in real life used to steal motorcycles as a boy

in his homeland of Scotland. Kim Coates, the Canadian who plays "Tig"—the triggerman and all-round scoundrel of the club—shared that in 1986, after totaling his bike, he promised his wife he would hang up his leathers and ride no more.

That didn't happen.

One interesting note was that the only cast member not to get a bike was Ron Perlman.

With Perlman in the role of the fictional club's president, "Clay," this obvious omission of felt especially mysterious at the time. However, a lot of that was cleared up when a 2010 *Los Angeles Times* article reported that the show's peevish patriarch was "the least comfortable on two wheels." The newspaper also quoted Perlman as saying, "I'm not wired for that kind of thrill. I'm intimidated by the size of [the bike], the power of it, the exposure of it." He also adds, "I really like my Mercedes with the Bose sound and the air conditioning and the fact that I can light a cigar and text message while I'm driving."

And there it is. No one can argue that an FXD is very different from an S-Class.

The Mechanics of Meticulousness who customized the bikes for SOA's Men of Mayhem.
Felicia Morgan

THE MECHANIC BEHIND THE MAN

It's a pretty cool thing to have a new bike to modify and personalize however you want—expenses be damned. But being assigned your own master wrench on top of that is almost like having Miss Teenage America for a cellmate.

Felicia details:

> After returning home to SoCal, each of the actors pondered their new toys and decided they needed a bit of tweaking. For some, it was as little as the addition of forward controls; for one, it was an additional fifty hours of change-outs!
>
> Eagle's Nest's baby-faced and polite Tanner Shackley, with a hand from fellow mechanic Russell, was responsible for handling Kurt Sutter's ride, which required the most detail work of all the bikes. Charlie "Hollywood" Peraino built Theo Rossi's ride. Russell Baugh, notorious for spontaneous burnouts on his personal bike, put Ryan Hurst's ride together. Chad Etter, known as "Chadillac," is the youngest of the crew and was responsible for the work on Charlie Hunnam's bike. William "Butch" Kerney, with scars to prove it, changed out Kim Coates' bike, which included a butt-load of spike nuts.
>
> Mike Foster took care of Tommy Flanagan's bike and installed glowing, multicolored fiber-optic engine lighting as a surprise for the actor. "Tiny" Rich Cundiff put the very specific details for Mark Boone's bike together for him.

I LOVE L.A.

A pack ride to Los Angeles with the mechanics on the new *SOA* scoots was next. No one seems to have fired shots at anyone behind the bunch (with their right *or* left hand), but a few of Randy Newman's lyrics were lived out once they reached L.A. Felicia continues:

> During the project, the mechanics developed a special bond with their assigned actor[s], each of whom was very genuine and appreciative of the work done by the crew. As a reward for all the hard work the wrenchers did over the course of the summer, Eagle's Nest H-D gave the crew a trip to "Beautiful Downtown Burbank" to personally present the completed bikes to the actors at the *SOA* studios.
>
> I was lucky enough to be invited along on what would be a whirlwind. An eight-hundred-some-mile-in-forty-odd-hours

PROP DEPT

"Next thing we knew, we were poking through the set of *Sons of Anarchy* completely unattended. Which means, like kids loose in their parent's bedroom, we snooped our asses off."
Felicia Morgan

turnaround trip to SoCal. An adrenaline-rush adventure that included a fourteen-motorcycle pack slicing rush hour traffic at breakneck speed on a Friday night in 105-degree weather through L.A. with the hillsides burning around us as we sucked up all the shit in the dingy gray skies.

After wiping the layer of soot from the nearby fires off our bikes the next morning, we cruised through the Burbank streets towards the studio. The short route included a nasty part of town that afforded us an opportunity to witness an arrest where the cops had a guy splayed against a wall as they patted him down and wrestled him into the cruiser. Then, just around the corner, a car was on fire in the middle of the boulevard.

Just another day in paradise.

INSIDE THE *SOA* SET

Alone on the *SOA* set, Felicia and the mechanics and the entourage were able to fire up the fantasy and, well, just plain snoop.

> We arrived at the gated *SOA* studio to discover that filming on location had gone on through the night and into the morning hours. We were told the actors would be meeting us as soon as humanly possible, so we set about entertaining ourselves by casually taking photos outside the buildings.
>
> Then the garage set was discovered.
>
> Next thing we knew, we were poking through the set of the *Sons of Anarchy* completely unattended. Which means, like kids loose in their parents' bedroom, we snooped our asses off. There was a general inventory taken on which things would really be found in a biker's home. Their staging included bottles of premium booze that few saddle tramps can really afford—nope, no Jack—and some riding paraphernalia. Most props were set up pretty well, but I'm here to tell you there was a complete lack of any genuine biker reading material. Not a single biker publication was found in the house set. Not an *Easyriders, In the Wind,* or *Thunder Press.* No J&P Cycles or any other parts catalogue, and no Orwell or *How to Build a Bonneville Salt Flats Motorcycle.* There were, however, magazines like *Sports Illustrated, Sunset,* and *Better Homes and Gardens.*
>
> Quick, someone call the ATF! Or maybe the Department of Agriculture! We kept exploring.
>
> There was climbing on the rather sticky stripper pole; hanging out in the club's bar; and some lounging on beds and pawing of certain props. Some wardrobe items were tried on. Everyone wandered their way through the silent and dark stage of the show in awe. No one tried to evict us. We were completely alone. By the time the weary pretend bikers started showing up, we'd managed to satisfy our *SOA* curiosity. As each actor arrived, they were shuttled off to the office for paperwork and formalities before getting a crash course in their bike's details with their mechanics.
>
> Sort of.
>
> Some didn't have their legal stuff together, some had no insurance, and some didn't have a motorcycle license. Since these motorcycles were intended to be the actors' personal bikes, not

meant for the show, these niggling little details caused some tense moments before it all got ironed out.

Several of the actors had a *few* problems adding smoothness to their skills, and the talk between them consisted of who dropped which bikes how many times on last year's show. But all were working hard at honing some riding finesse; however, I didn't expect anyone to be in Jason Pullen's category anytime soon—or maybe ever.

When Kurt Sutter was asked what his wife, Katey Sagal, thought of the new motorcycle and all that the show entails, he looked off in the distance, shook his head, and said, "Right now, she wishes I was writing for CSI."

EPILOGUE: THE FXDS' FAREWELL PERFORMANCES

Felicia wraps up:

> Initially, the riding community was disgusted that the show was not real, and folks were picking it apart over authenticity. The dealership's goal was to help the guys and the series by getting them closer to what they were portraying.
>
> Of course, the dealer got some good, positive promotion for their work and hardware, too. And they imposed some restrictions that included a year of riding before the actors could either turn the bikes back in or purchase them outright.
>
> Not all the guys ended up keeping the bikes. Ryan Hurst was the most visibly nervous about the whole thing—and the least impressed. Charlie, Kim, and Tommy did buy theirs, although "bad boy" Tommy totaled his, getting a "little scuffed up" in the process!
>
> Theo Rossi, who wasn't a seasoned rider, went on to have a custom bike built, and he continues to ride to this day, so we got at least one convert to our team!

And as the road rolled on, there were more.

That 2010 *Los Angeles Times* article also stated that Mark Boone "now rides every day, as does Hunnam, who says he's put 7,500 miles on his Harley in the past year."

Felicia Morgan's and the *Times*' chronicles of SAMCRO at a real street level clear up some of the myths, mysteries, and rumors as to whether or not the actors could ride, but it also adds to them. Some may have bikes—but years after the final season splat, do any of these guys ever wake up in the middle of the night, nervous and twitching with a need for a moonless solo ride *somewhere*? Do they ever need the kind of healing rush that they spent seven television seasons injecting into the vicarious veins of a shaky public—a public that will never, ever mainline even a small jagged slice of the lifestyle these guys portrayed?

REACTION AND RESPONSE

It's true: a culture-caring and concerned NorCal H-D dealer arranged to get the *SOA* boys bikes of their own in the hopes that some "method acting" might bring the series closer to reality. And the gesture may have worked. While not all of them could ride, or even had the desire to, a few definitely seem to have become converts to our team.

PART VII

Conclusion Confusion

CHAPTER 30:

WACO

PERHAPS THE BIGGEST MYSTERY OF ALL

INTERROGATING THE SUBJECT

Nine dead and no real answers?

> Gunfire erupted Sunday among rival biker gangs in Waco, Texas,
> leaving at least nine people dead, according to police.
> —CNN, May 17, 2015

Nine dead.

> A white gunman opened fire Wednesday night at a historic black
> church in downtown Charleston, S.C., killing nine people before
> fleeing and setting off an overnight manhunt, the police said.
> —*The New York Times*, June 17, 2015

Nine dead.

E xactly one month apart, two horrible shootings bloodied the southern
United States.

But they were very different.

The timeline in the South Carolina shooting shows that by 10:44 a.m. on
June 18, the morning after the killings, the killer had been not only identified but
captured about two hundred forty-five miles from the murder scene. Also on June 18,
President Barack Obama made his way quickly to Charleston to offer condolences
and to make a plea for gun control: "Once again, innocent people were killed, in part
because someone who wanted to inflict harm had no trouble getting their hands on a
gun . . . We as a country will have to reckon with the fact that this type of mass violence
does not happen in other advanced countries."

One day after *that*, the United States Department of Justice fast-tracked a Crime
Victim Assistance Formula Grant of $29 million to South Carolina, with portions of the
money given to the survivors.

The suspect, twenty-one-year-old Dylann Roof, was rapidly indicted on thirty-
three federal hate crime charges.

By the time Independence Day rolled around a few weeks after the crime, the
historical battle flag of the Confederate States of America—apparently a favorite totem
of Roof's—has been removed, buried, and banned in Southern state houses, Wal-Mart,
Amazon, Sears, and Kmart and scratched from the hardtop of *The Dukes of Hazzard's* '69
Dodge Charger, the *General Lee*.

Meanwhile, the wheels of Waco justice have turned somewhat slower.

BULLETS AND BEDLAM

A quick recap of what went down in central Texas's most notorious town begins at the Twin Peaks restaurant, where a regular monthly meeting of the Texas Confederation of Clubs and Independents (COC&I) was being held. According to police, at a little after noon, an argument started between members of two clubs over "a parking spot where someone had their foot run over."

At 12:24, the argument turned to bullets and bedlam.

And here's where tangible truths take the real hit. It didn't take long for nine people to be killed and eighteen more wounded. Upwards of 170 people (177 is the generally accepted total) were arrested in a wholesale roundup and held on a million dollars bail each. Bikes were herded onto flatbed trucks like scrap metal—about 135, according to local news, along with about eighty cars and pickups—which "through civil forfeiture law, may be auctioned off by the county, regardless of whether or not their owners are convicted."

Ironically, the COC&I had been honored by the city council of Jacksonville just three days before the shootings for its involvement in Motorcycle Safety and Awareness Month. The award notwithstanding, some members of the confederation had now lost their lives, their vehicles, and/or a potentially great deal of freedom-time in a prohibitive-bail jail.

IN PLACE, LYING IN WAIT?

The South Carolina church killings brought fast answers. Waco brought grating, stagnating questions.

One of the most troubling was why there was a large battery of local and state officers already at the restaurant; all SWATed up in tactical gear and "in place" long before the meeting. Police said it was because they had been made aware that a turf war was brewing and that it might just blow. But the militarily intimidating show of might added to the post-shooting feelings that the police had been more than itching for a confrontation—or, as some have put it, lying in wait.

Another biting and uneasy non-answer concerns just who shot whom. Month after month went by with no ballistics report. (The entire United States Constitution was written in just four months—including that awkward part about a "speedy trial.")

> After almost five months, the criminal justice system in Waco
> continues to mystify journalists and legal minds across the nation
> with more questions arising than answers. Observers are impatiently
> awaiting the elusive ballistics report that will say once and for all
> if this was truly a biker-on-biker crime, a cop-on-biker crime, or a

combination thereof that left nine motorcyclists lying in pools of blood in a parking lot on a beautiful Sunday afternoon.
—Raine Devries, russbrown.com blog, October 9, 2015

The autopsy reports dragged on as well, kicking in even more questions:

It would be four full months before the autopsy report would be released on the nine slain motorcyclists. The report clearly states that five were shot in the head, neck, and/or back with "downward trajectory" and one had a bullet hole in the top of his head; those men were possibly on their knees when shot and none of them had evidence of debris, indicating that they were shot at close range.

One man was shot in the buttocks and thigh...he died by bleeding out in that parking lot within sight of a hospital just across the road. Waco police officers reportedly would not allow paramedics to tend to his wounds nor would they allow fellow motorcyclists with military combat experience to help him. According to those at the scene, those officers clearly and loudly told the bikers trying to help the dead and dying that they were to lie facedown or they too would be shot.
—Raine Devries, russbrown.com blog, October 9, 2015

More myths, mysteries, and rumors eat away at the carcass of Waco by way of the rotting, nepotistic teeth of the local bureaucracy. The district attorney and the judge who eventually issued a gag order over all the official information were former law partners. A Waco police detective was appointed as foreman of the grand jury hearing the cases of the one-hundred-seventy-plus who were arrested.

SOUNDS THAT ARE IMPOSSIBLE TO FORGET
But one of the toughest mysteries to dodge is that of the big-gun firepower that seems to have packed the main mow-down punch—firepower that the bikers just didn't have.

WACO, Texas (AP)—First came a few pistol shots, several witnesses said, then a barrage of rifle fire during the shootout last month at a Waco restaurant favored by bikers. But authorities still have not said how many of the dead and wounded were the result of police fire.

Police have identified only one assault weapon, a semi-automatic gun that fires high-powered ammunition, among the

firearms confiscated from bikers, and that was found in a locked
car after the shooting ended. But several witnesses—at least three
of them veterans with weapons training—told The Associated Press
that semi-automatic gunfire dominated the May 17 shootout that
left nine dead and 18 wounded.

—Emily Schmall, Associated Press, June 6, 2015

The small-environment, "box canyon"–like parking lot of the restaurant may have
also been a factor in the deaths. Blogger Raine Devries commented, "Witnessing how
small [the parking lot] is forces the realization that those bikers were shot like fish in a
barrel with nowhere to escape."

News photos of bikes on their sides in that parking lot, apparently knocked over in
the close quarters of the melee, were chilling.

"IS IT POSSIBLE? YES. IS IT A FACT? NO."

Known as the public face of the Waco Police Department, Sergeant W. Patrick Swanton
was in full press-conference mode directly after the incident.

He was also the omnipresent voice.

His comments were many, with rhetoric steeped in everything from politically
smooth spin to sensationalistic scene setting to vindictiveness for the biker vermin
crawling around his town.

Of the cops and who-shot-whom he said:

Eighteen uniformed Waco police officers including an assistant chief,
sergeants and one rookie were standing by outside the restaurant
Sunday and responded within a matter of seconds after the violence
broke out between members of five rival gangs . . . They did a hell of
job in response to a very deadly scene. . . .

Our officers took fire and responded appropriately, returning
fire. . . .

The number of shots fired and who fired them won't be released
immediately, pending completion of the investigation. . . .

Those officers quickly gained control of a very violent scene and
took numerous biker individuals into temporary custody. . . .

Swanton discounted media reports that four of the nine bikers were killed by
police, saying:

[T]hat will be impossible to determine until autopsies and ballistic tests have been completed...Is it possible? Yes. Is it a fact? No....

They've found evidence of some type of altercation inside, including blood...We will figure it out...We do know that we have crime scenes inside and outside and we know that assaults occurred inside and outside the establishment...The eighteen Waco officers and four Texas Department of Public Safety Officers involved in the incident remain on duty as Waco police, Texas Rangers and the DPS Criminal Investigation Division investigate.

Swanton made the scene come ironically alive:

There's blood splatter—blood evidence—everywhere; there's still food on the tables, half-eaten hamburgers, half-drunk margaritas. It's the most surreal thing I've ever seen...There are still purses on the table from a small number of citizens...Blood still on the parking lot is an environmental issue at this point.

We're talking unimaginable numbers of evidence that we're going to have to lift from this crime scene...The shooting investigation will take weeks if not months...

Welcome to Central Texas's most notorious town. *Jennifer Thomas*

Swanton confirmed that there had been "credible threats to law enforcement in and around our area" but said those have toned down. "We're thankful for that," he said.

> Patrol officers have arrested a few bikers in the area and report that they are seeing fewer bikers Tuesday . . . The violent feud likely hasn't ended, though . . . Is this over? Most likely not . . . We would like it to be. Would like some sort of truce. . . .
>
> Waco crime scene investigators assisted by officers from federal, state and county agencies including the FBI, the ATF and the Department of Public Safety, were meticulously diagramming the crime scene Monday [the day after the shootings] . . . Once that process is finished, about one hundred motorcycles and many of the fifty to seventy-five private vehicles in the restaurant's parking lot will be towed away as evidence.

However, Swanton said the restaurant's owners were not cooperative with police. "They have some answering not only to do to you, but to our community as well," he told reporters.

He declined to name the gangs, saying, "We're not going to give them publicity."

AFTER THE AFTERMATH

Twin Peaks Waco never served another beer or burger. The place was snap-stripped of its licenses and signs and now sits vacant with bullet holes and a makeshift memorial of nine yellow skulls.

Sergeant W. Patrick Swanton, however, was still cookin' with gas.

On July 27, 2015, the gregarious and gracious officer announced he will run for sheriff of McLennan County, the number-one law enforcement office in the land of Waco. His big news came as the "fair trials" of those jailed and facing fifteen-to-life, and justice for those killed and wounded in the Waco shootings, lingered and limped along like crippled armadillos out on I-40.

REACTION AND RESPONSE

Indeed, sure answers as to just what really occurred that day in Waco—and why—may never be fully revealed. But maybe more important are the questions that surround the lack of rapid legal action, the wholesale arrest of so many people just because they were there, the seizure of so many innocents' vehicles, and the complete disruption—and in some cases, destruction—of their lives.

EPILOGUE

IF YOU FEAR SOMETHING ENOUGH, YOU CAN MAKE IT HAPPEN

Waco and its investigation fell steeply and quickly into a sodden culvert, becoming a plodding, convoluted mess that—like Laughlin 2002 and other "incidents"—may never see any solid resolution.

But it's much more than a murder mystery.

It epitomizes so many of the kinds of myths, mysteries, and rumors that have permeated the biker and one-percenter culture forever, ones that have been aimed at every aspect of the lifestyle: runs, clothes, race, international spread and influence, cops and the law, the machines, and even fear.

And that last one might just be the biggie.

A very frightening axiom came from the movie about the seriously troubled '60s writer Sylvia Plath: "If you fear something enough, you can make it happen."

That may be what happened in Waco.

Nervous fear and a "lying in wait" edginess shown toward bikers may have been the real trigger. The corralling and long-term, budget-busting detainment of one hundred seventy-seven people was an obvious and head-shaking overreaction.

But overreaction is common when myths, mysteries, and rumors are infused with fear.

It's what has caused abuses of another of those awkward parts of the constitution: freedom of assembly and association. Big nets for bikers were thrown out in Waco just because they happened to be with other bikers. The same kinds of roundups and prohibitions have occurred over and over in US federal cases and internationally in places like Australia.

Luckily, however, as big as those nets are, they will never hook the entire culture. A lust and love for freedom and individuality apart from the mainstream mundane will slip any trap.

And that is no mystery.

ACKNOWLEDGMENTS

The term *brotherhood* is often thrown around and deflated like Tom Brady's balls, but a few people in this lifestyle still genuinely understand one of its meanings: that of helping out, sacrificing, and contributing to the positive image of a culture that forever has had a big target on its back. I would like to thank those true brothers—and sisters—who aided me with this book. No project about the biker or one-percenter culture should or could be done by one person. The biker community should be just that: a *community*, with collective and individual voices that all count and have an impact.

My sincere gratitude goes out to:

The two best and hippest editors and "book people" in the world, my wife, Jennifer Thomas, and Motorbooks' Darwin Holmstrom; "Tramp" from Wheels of Soul MC; film producer Randall Wilson; "Spike," nomad, longtime member, and former "P" of the OCMC of the Hessians MC; "Seeker of the Sacred," Bo Bushnell; Clay Jones, "P" of China's Long March MC; Lommel, "P" of Germany's Born to be Wild MC; Michael Schacht of the Crocker Motorcycle Company; Felicia Morgan, photojournalist and iron-butt rider extraordinaire; the late William "Sweet William" "Tumbleweed" Fritsch; San Francisco's and India's Miles Davis; and blogger/activist Raine Devries.

And a special thanks to "Knuckles," "Reno," and "Preacher" for helping me to keep believing in that elusive ideal of brotherhood.

INDEX

237

238

239